GRAND ENDEAVORS

OF AMERICAN INDIAN PHOTOGRAPHY

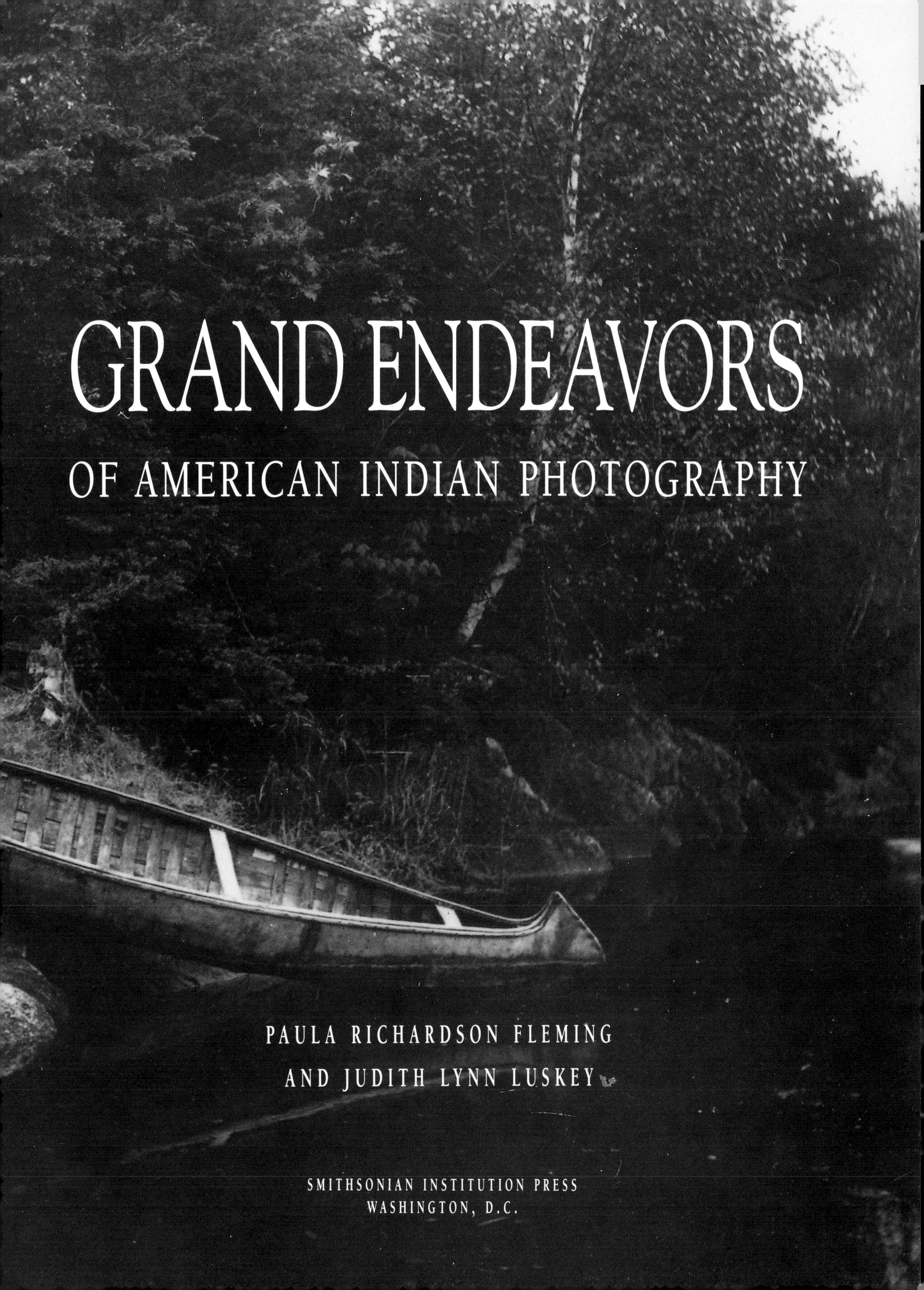

GRAND ENDEAVORS

OF AMERICAN INDIAN PHOTOGRAPHY

PAULA RICHARDSON FLEMING

AND JUDITH LYNN LUSKEY

SMITHSONIAN INSTITUTION PRESS
WASHINGTON, D.C.

FRONTISPIECE
'The Portage'
Chippewa canoes in Minnesota.
ROLAND REED

PAGE EIGHT
The famous Chiricahua Apache chief Geronimo, photographed
at the Louisiana Purchase Exposition in 1904.
GERHARD SISTERS

© *1993 Paula Richardson Fleming and Judith Lynn Luskey*
All rights reserved

Published in the United States by Smithsonian Institution Press
Library of Congress Catalog Number 93–83451
ISBN 1–56098–297–7

This book was designed and produced by Calmann & King Ltd, London

Designed by Karen Stafford, DQP, London
Photographic research by Paula Richardson Fleming and Judith Lynn Luskey
Typeset in Horley by Tek-Art, Addiscombe, Croydon, Surrey
Origination by Eray Scan
Printed in Hong Kong

Contents

Acknowledgments   6

Map   7

Introduction   11

Chapter 1   EARLY GRAND ENDEAVORS   17

Chapter 2   INDEPENDENT MASTER PHOTOGRAPHERS   29

Chapter 3   EXPOSITIONS AND WORLD FAIRS   77

Chapter 4   THE PICTORIALISTS   99

Footnotes   171

Picture Credits   172

Bibliography   173

Index   175

Acknowledgments

As with any book, the help of many supports the work of a few. This publication is no exception. Without the assistance of the people listed below, this work would never have been produced. We gratefully acknowledge their backing.

Approval was received from the Smithsonian Institution to allow us to proceed with our own grand endeavor. A special note of thanks is offered to Dr Donald J. Ortner, Chairman, Department of Anthropology; Dr Mary Elizabeth Ruwell, Director, National Anthropological Archives; Jim Wilson, Assistant General Counsel, Smithsonian Institution; Dan Goodwin and Amy Pastan, Smithsonian Institution Press.

We received professional support and encouragement from many individuals. Of special note are: Dr Tom Kavanagh, Jerry Kerns, Lynn Mitchell, Alison Devine Nordstrom, Fr. Peter Powell, Dr Richard Rudisill, Tom Southall and Tex Treadwell. For their continued inspiration, even long distance, a special mention must be made of our mentors, Dr Waldo Wedel, Mildred Mott Wedel and Dr John C. Ewers.

Mr Leon Kramer of the Kramer Gallery, St Paul, Minnesota, should get a special award for providing us with the stunning photographs by Roland Reed. Many museums and historical societies provided us with other beautiful photographs to grace these pages. They include John Carter and Martha Miller, Nebraska State Historical Society; Kimberly Cody, National Museum of American Art; Mary Kay Davies and Leslie Overstreet, Smithsonian Institution Libraries; Barbara Mathe, American Museum of Natural History; Duane Sneddeker and Kirsten Hammerstron, Missouri Historical Society; and the staffs of the Alaska State Library, the Milwaukee Public Museum, and the Smithsonian Institution National Anthropological Archives.

Prints for the majority of the illustrations were provided by the Smithsonian Institution Office of Printing and Photographic Services. Individuals who were particularly helpful include David Burgevin, Joyce Goulait, Alan Hart, Vic Krantz, Mary Ellen McCaffrey, Nick Parrella, Terri Sprouell, Doc Dougherty and an added thank you to Louie Thomas.

This book was conceived by Laurence King, of Calmann & King Ltd. Without his vision, these beautiful images would not have been brought together. We thank him for his continued support and foresight. We also wish to thank Sophie Collins, Senior Editor, who was especially helpful in the early formation of the work, and Jacky Colliss Harvey, our ever-patient editor, who displayed a wonderful sense of humor and understanding throughout the production and standard last-minute problems. We also thank Karen Stafford, our designer, for her work.

Finally, a word of thanks must be said to all the friends and families who kept us fed, happy and inspired during the writing of this book, especially Edward Donnen and family, Maxine Donnen, Agnes and Irving Luskey (in memoriam), Marion and Norton Richardson, the Snarbis families and Dianne Walker. We would also like to thank Giggle and Foop for faxes and emergency computer services, Kevin Haslag and Elaine Snow, Michal Mainwaring, Fahrney's Pens, Sunita Gupta, and last but not least, the denizens of the Childe Harold and the Old Mythical.

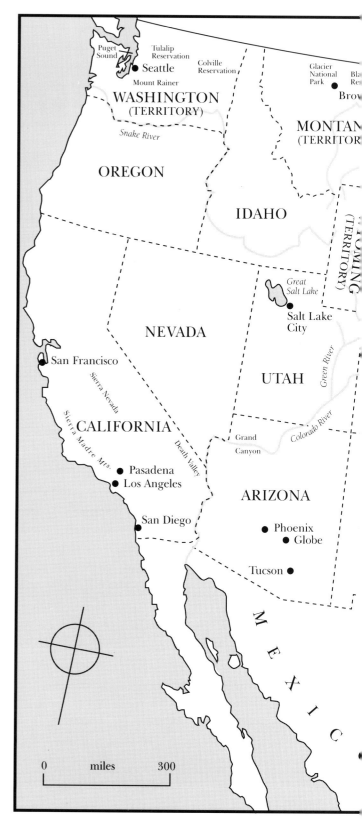

This map primarily indicates locations mentioned in the text. Many regions were territories before becoming states. As boundaries sometimes changed, a modern map has been used for ease of reference.

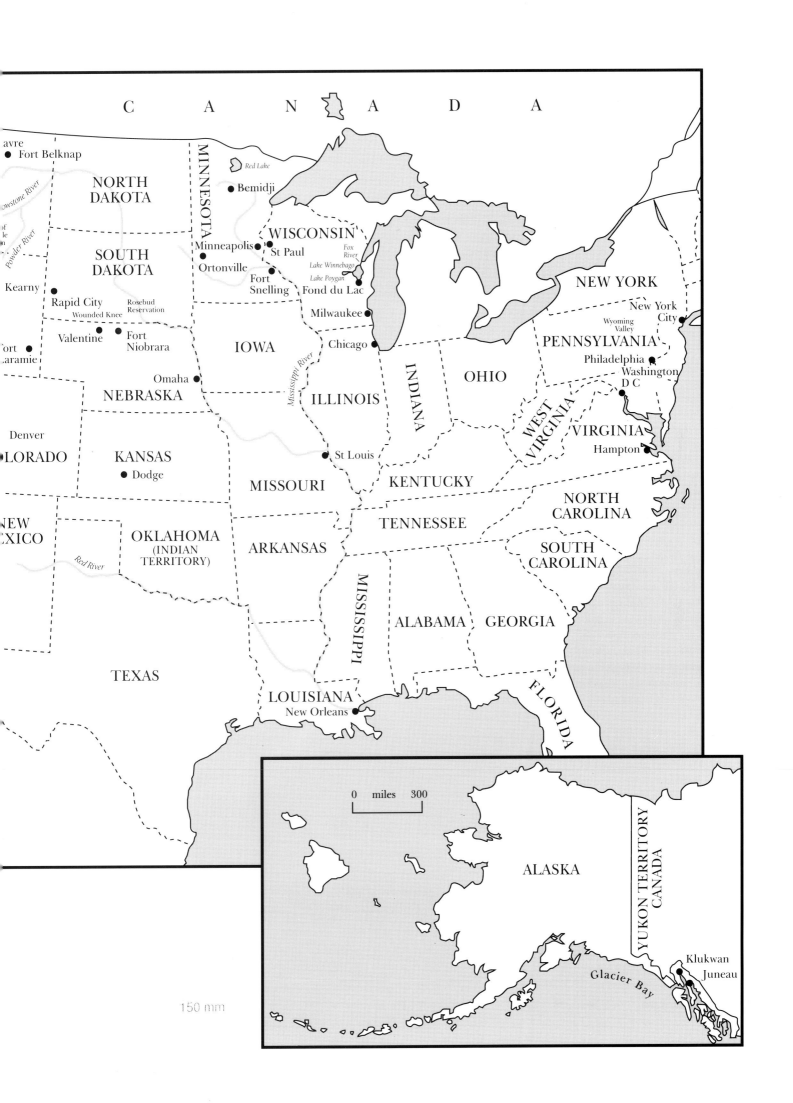

CANADA

Havre
● Fort Belknap

Yellowstone River

NORTH DAKOTA

MINNESOTA

Red Lake

● Bemidji

Powder River

SOUTH DAKOTA

WISCONSIN

Minneapolis ●   St Paul ●

Fox River

Ortonville ●

Lake Winnebago
Lake Poygan

Fort Snelling ●   Fond du Lac ●

Kearny ●

Rapid City ●   Rosebud Reservation

Wounded Knee

Milwaukee ●

IOWA

Valentine ●   Fort Niobrara ●

Mississippi River

Chicago ●

NEW YORK

New York City ●

Wyoming Valley

PENNSYLVANIA

Fort Laramie ●

Omaha ●

NEBRASKA

ILLINOIS   INDIANA   OHIO

Philadelphia ●
Washington D C ●

Denver

COLORADO   KANSAS

St Louis ●

WEST VIRGINIA   VIRGINIA

Hampton ●

● Dodge

MISSOURI   KENTUCKY

NEW MEXICO

OKLAHOMA (INDIAN TERRITORY)

Red River

ARKANSAS

TENNESSEE

NORTH CAROLINA

SOUTH CAROLINA

MISSISSIPPI

ALABAMA   GEORGIA

TEXAS

LOUISIANA

New Orleans ●

FLORIDA

0   miles   300

ALASKA

YUKON TERRITORY
CANADA

Klukwan ●
Juneau ●

Glacier Bay

150 mm

"Geronimo"
copyright by
Gerhard Sisters
St. Louis Mo.

Introduction

'What can be more melancholy than their history? By a law of their nature, they seem destined to a slow, but sure extinction. Everywhere, at the approach of the white man, they fade away. We hear the rustling of their footsteps, like that of the withered leaves of autumn, and they are gone for ever. They pass mournfully by us, and they return no more.'[1]

The North American Indians, as a vanishing race, have captured the imaginations of Euro-Americans ever since it became apparent that the creation of a new country was having a profound effect upon the lives of the Native Americans. The nineteenth-century doctrine of Manifest Destiny had maintained that the United States had both a right and a duty to expand throughout the whole of the North American continent, but this came to be increasingly offset by a new concern for these vanishing cultures, a concern that was expressed in many forms, from personal diaries to scientific reports. If the Indians themselves could not be preserved, then, it was felt, at least their lifestyles could be documented.

Reacting to the image of the doomed American Indian, countless writers and artists recorded these vanishing races in paintings, descriptions and photographs. The point of view which comes across in these works, however, ranges from nostalgia for the noble red man, to support for the elimination of bloodthirsty savages in the name of civilization.

Obviously, both Indians and settlers wanted to control their own lives and their own destinies, and skirmishes inevitably led to war. Both sides were right; both sides were wrong. Newspaper accounts of frontier wars and the stories of settlers who had experienced life on the frontier helped strengthen the biased idea of the bloodthirsty savage in particular.

Obtaining the images to illustrate these narratives was in itself a problem. The technical considerations of wet- and dry-plate photography meant that even if a photographer happened to be in the right place at the right time, with his equipment already set up, he still could not make instant images, nor record the motion of a skirmish. He could also find himself in very considerable danger. Many frontier photographers found that they needed to travel with military forces for protection, and even that was no guarantee of safety. The frontier photographer Ridgway Glover, describing his experiences with the Indians in a series of letters published in the *Philadelphia Photographer* in 1866, wrote that 'They [the Indians] looked very wild and savage-like while galloping around us; and I desired to make some instantaneous views, but our commander ordered me not to, as he expected an attack at any time . . . They attacked our train in the rear, killed two of the privates, and lost two of their number.'[2] Not long after, there was an editorial note in the same magazine: 'Mr. Ridgway Glover was killed near Fort Phil Kearny on the 14th of September by the Sioux Indians. He was scalped, killed, and horribly mutilated.'[3]

Sitting Bull, a Hunkpapa Dakota, in 1885.
DAVID F. BARRY

Photograph of a Shoshoni man and woman, sold bearing captions such as 'Venus and Adonis'. This image was circulated by Savage and Ottinger of Salt Lake City, and Edric Eaton of Omaha, Nebraska, among others, in the 1860s and 1870s.

A further complication during this early period was the fact that publications could not reproduce photographs, and had to rely upon artists' interpretations of events, which were then turned into line engravings. The illustrator James E. Taylor based his drawings for magazines on photographic portraits whenever possible, but nonetheless still had to rely upon his own artistry to delineate a scene in its entirety. No doubt his goal was to produce as accurate a reconstruction of an event as possible, but images such as his depiction of the aftermath of an Indian attack only helped foster the perception of Indians as uncivilized savages, as is shown by a contemporary review of his work — '. . . the series of illustrations by Mr. James E. Taylor, [represents] the Indians in their favorite amusements, such as scalping, torturing, murdering, mutilating and fighting . . . The pictures have also a tendency to cause us to believe that the best kind of Indian is a dead Indian.'[4]

The Indians were popularly viewed as subhuman, and thus as appropriate subjects for low humor. Photographs of a Shoshoni man and woman, bearing the caption 'Venus and Adonis', were circulated in the 1860s and 1870s by the photographers Savage and Ottinger and Edric Eaton. Words such as 'buck' entered the English language. Although originally the shortened version of 'buckskin', a unit of trade with the Indians, it quickly became more commonly associated with the noun referring to the adult male of some species of animal.[5] Such views of the Native Americans remained popular as long as the Indians were seen as savage and threatening.

In 1890 the massacre at Wounded Knee brought a virtual end to the Indian wars. That same year, the Census Bureau included US territories in the census for the first time, signaling the end of the frontier. Railroads crisscrossed the country, and with both accessibility and safety thus guaranteed, the American West became a popular subject for artists and photographers alike. The end of the Indian as an ethnic entity was accepted as inevitable. 'The buffalo were gone, the land was fenced, the people were living in unfamiliar square houses, the eagle was caged and dying.'[6] This concept of the Indians became the driving force behind many photographers and anthropologists, who realized the necessity of recording Indian culture as quickly as possible. The technological difficulties of early photography meant that most frontier photographers were professionals, and regardless of any other motivations they may have had for recording the Indians, most needed to make a profit from their work. Thus photographers tended to amass large collections of negatives more by accretion than according to any very defined goal. During the late nineteenth century, however, vast changes occurred in photographic technology. Glass-plate negatives and large-format cameras were replaced by box cameras and roll film. Kodak's inventions had put fifty thousand photographers on the scene almost overnight, and photography was no longer the domain of the professional.[7] Combined with the desire to record the traditional lifestyles of the Indians, this encouraged many photographers to embark upon 'grand endeavors' – conscious efforts, whose primary purpose was accurate documentation, not simple profit.

This ideal influenced several generations of photographers, who viewed themselves as visual historians. Frederick Monsen's response was typical:

'I began my work among them [the Indians] twenty-two years ago, and have seen many changes. Entire tribes have been destroyed by disease, and others have been scattered by encroaching civilization. The Indian, as an Indian, is rapidly disappearing. He is adopting the white man's ways and losing his tribal characteristics. He is gradually giving up his deeply significant nature-lore, his religions and his ceremonies, ancestral manners and customs will have passed from his life.

Realizing these conditions, I have devoted many years to the making of an ethnographic record of the Indians, photographing their life, manners and habitat, and thus preserving for future generations, a picture-history which will show what these most interesting early Americans were like, before they were disturbed by the influences of the white man.'[8]

At the same time, America celebrated its growth and accomplishments with a series of expositions. The Indians were now part of the history of a rapidly growing nation. No longer threats to settlement, they took part in the expositions as 'living exhibitions', documenting the nation's growth. They also thrilled audiences at Wild West shows, as reminders of how life had been on the former frontier. Ethnologists such as James Mooney hoped to use these expositions as a means of educating their audiences about Native American life, while at the same time taking advantage of the opportunity to document the Indians photographically. Unfortunately, activities such as sham battles degenerated into free-for-alls, severely limiting their educational value; but, photographically, several grand endeavors of note were created, such as the series of Indian portraits produced by Frank Rinehart and Adolph Muhr at the Trans-Mississippi and International Exposition in 1898, and those taken by the Gerhard sisters at the St Louis World's Fair in 1904.

Due to the tens of thousands of Kodak-toting amateurs, professional photographers had to invent techniques and viewpoints that would enable them to create images beyond those possible with the new snapshot technology. Art salons were organized, devoted to more aesthetic styles of photography. The photographers who exhibited in them were known as 'Pictorialists', and attempted to recreate the effects of Impressionist paintings. Dramatic close-ups and lighting, soft-focus and tinting were all used to create their romantic views, and what better romantic theme could there be than that of the American Indian, fading away before the onslaught of civilization?[9] The fact that the earlier dangers and inconveniences of frontier travel had been removed made the idea all the more appealing. But in turning their lenses on the American Indian, the photographers soon realized that the reality of Indian life was less than romantic perfection. Assuming the Indian to have once been noble, 'The key to reconciling expectation and actuality was in building backward from the present reality to the past ideal.'[10] Photographers such as Joseph Kossuth Dixon, on the Wanamaker Expeditions, and Roland Reed used this new artistic approach in their grand endeavors, but the ultimate example of its use is found in the work of Edward S. Curtis, who devoted almost thirty years of his life to creating a masterly record of the North American Indian.

It would be wrong to assume that all the photographers who took as their subjects the American Indians were masters of their art, and in fact only a small percentage produced exceptional photographs. The intention of this book is to look more closely at some of these masterworks, to give an insight into the lives of the photographers who created them, and most importantly to allow the reader to appreciate their beauty, which raises them beyond the considerations of technical craftsmanship to become art.

The criteria for assessing masterpieces are as varied as the opinions of those assessing them. The authors have made their selection to show variations of approach, different Indian cultures and simple personal preferences. Many noteworthy photographers, such as David F. Barry and Frank J. Haynes, have largely been omitted, as their photographs are readily available in other publications. Some, such as Edward S. Curtis, have been the subject of many publications, but as their works epitomize the grand endeavor, they must be included. The authors have, however, sought to represent them by including some lesser-known works, in place, perhaps, of the most familiar icons of North American Indian photography. We have also included the works of some photographers known mostly only to specialists, in the hope of presenting their photographs in the light of a new artistic merit. Our wish is to broaden the awareness of those photographers whose masterpieces have been overshadowed by the work of more celebrated artists, while still appreciating the great contributions made by acknowledged masters.

This work is not intended to provide anthropological or ethnographical interpretations, nor an in-depth study of each photographer's work. For those readers who are interested in learning more about individual photographers, a bibliography is included as a starting point toward more detailed research.

Modern photographic paper and printing techniques can only approximate the warm, delicate tones and fine surfaces of the originals. Nonetheless, in order to reveal the maximum detail and beauty of these images, original glass-plate or film negatives have been used whenever possible. In the absence of original negatives, copy negatives have been made from vintage originals.

We have produced this book to honor the 'shadow catchers', who devoted their careers and their lives to recording the Indians. We honor, most of all, the North American Indians themselves. It is their history; through this book we want to return a part of it to them. We, like the photographers, dedicate this endeavor to the future generations, and to the Indians who did not vanish after all.

Illustration taken from one of James Earle Taylor's original drawings, entitled 'Aftermath of an Indian attack', and dated 1886. A contemporary review of Taylor's work stated sarcastically that 'We have never seen more spirited pictures of the doings of the noble red man . . .' Images such as these helped foster stereotyped views of the Indians.

Chief Joseph of the Nez Perce, photographed circa 1877. Circulated by Frank J. Haynes, Orlando Scott Goff, and Goff's protégé, David F. Barry. Photographers such as Barry and Haynes created significant collections of images of the American Indian during their careers, but we do not always know if they set out to record Indian life on a grand scale, or simply amassed their collections through time. Moreover, many augmented their own works by acquiring images by other photographers, thus proper attribution can also be difficult.

Navaho Indians in the Canyon de Chelley, Arizona, 1904. Images such as Curtis's 'The Vanishing Race' (a group of Indians riding off into the sunset), or this view in the Canyon de Chelley have become icons of American Indian photography. The impact of his work has been so widespread that to most people his name is synonymous with Indian photography.
EDWARD S. CURTIS

Early
Grand
Endeavors

NEW LAND. New opportunities. New freedoms. Such dreams inspired countless settlers to spread west across the American continent, fired with a sense of making a better life for themselves. Yet this 'winning' of the American West was all to be accomplished at the expense of the American Indians.

The recurring theme of the vanishing North American Indians reached its peak in the late nineteenth century, with the increasingly rapid changes to the American West and to Indian life. These changes gave an extra sense of urgency to the work of turn-of-the-century photographers, but their work itself was not conceptually new, and followed earlier artistic and photographic endeavors.

GEORGE CATLIN

The most famous of these early nineteenth-century artists was George Catlin, who considered himself lucky to have been born '... in time to see these people in their native dignity, and beauty, and independence'.[1]

Catlin was born in 1796. His own mother and grandmother had briefly been captured by Miami Indians in the Wyoming Valley Pennsylvania massacre of 1778, an incident which provided a source of inspiration for Catlin's adolescent sketching.[2] Although he initially worked as a lawyer, he soon abandoned that career and dedicated his life to art. By the early 1820s he had won a reputation as an important artist, but was still 'continually reaching for some branch or enterprise of the art, on which to devote a whole lifetime of enthusiasm.'[3] The visit of an Indian delegation to the town of Philadelphia provided just the spark he needed to inspire his artistic passion. As he recalled:

'I have, for many years past, contemplated the noble races of red men who are now spread over these trackless forests and boundless prairies, melting away at the approach of civilization. Their rights invaded, their morals corrupted, their lands wrested from them, their customs changed, and therefore lost to the world; and they at last sunk into the earth, and the ploughshare turning the sod over their graves, and I have flown to their rescue – not of their lives or of their race (for they are "doomed" and must perish), but to the rescue of their looks and their modes, at which the acquisitive world

Portrait of No Heart, an Iowa, by Charles Bird King, 1837. One of the paintings of visiting Indian delegates to Washington DC made at the behest of Colonel Thomas L. McKenney. No Heart's skill and ruthlessness in battle, and the contempt with which he viewed life, his own or his enemies', had earned him his name. Eventually he chose to seek peace by other means, and in 1837 was in Washington to make a treaty.

may hurl their poison and every besom of destruction, and trample them down and crush them to death; yet, phoenix-like again upon canvass [*sic*], and stand forth for centuries yet to come, the living monuments of a noble race. For this purpose, I have designed to visit every tribe of Indians on the Continent, if my life should be spared; for the purpose of procuring portraits of distinguished Indians, of both sexes in each tribe, painted in their native costume; accompanied with pictures of their villages, domestic habits, games, mysteries, religious ceremonies, etc. with anecdotes, traditions, and history of their respective nations.'[4]

To turn this grand endeavor into reality, Catlin needed financial support. Colonel William F. Stone, a New York publisher, financed Catlin's first trip west aboard the steamboat *Yellowstone*, on its maiden journey up the Missouri River in 1832. By late 1836 Catlin had completed over four hundred paintings and thousands of sketches among at least forty-eight tribes, almost completing his 'Indian Gallery'. The financial costs, however, were substantial.

In 1837 Catlin took his gallery on the road, in the hope of recouping his losses and gaining a permanent museum for his work. His first major exhibit, which opened that year in New York City, was immensely popular and began to make Catlin's name synonymous with paintings of American Indians. Unfortunately his lack of business acumen resulted in costs exceeding admission fees.[5]

In 1839, after the government had refused to purchase his collection, Catlin took his show to Europe, where he hoped to enhance his reputation and acquire a new market. He landed at Liverpool with eight tons of luggage, including over six hundred paintings, Indian artifacts, a pair of live grizzly bears, two dozen mannequins dressed in Indian costumes and eventually the Indians themselves.[6] The artist had turned showman.

Catlin's tour around Europe was immensely popular, and gained the support of many influential people. Even so, in 1849, the United States Congress again decided against purchasing his paintings. As the costs of his touring gallery mounted, Catlin tried many schemes to raise money, such as the publication of his field notes and the production of lithographs of his more popular paintings. Nonetheless, he fell heavily into debt, and by 1852 his collection was in danger of being seized and divided among his European creditors. Catlin was saved by Joseph Harrison, a wealthy American boiler-maker, who purchased the paintings and had them shipped back to Philadelphia.

Catlin himself returned to the United States in 1870, penniless, over seventy, and alone – his wife and only son had died and his daughters had already been sent back to America.[7] But his enthusiasm for documenting the American Indians was undaunted, and was to create yet one more exhibition of his paintings, to which he invited a friend, William Henry Blackmore, an English entrepreneur. Deeply impressed, Blackmore persuaded another friend, Joseph Henry, the Secretary of the Smithsonian Institution, to invite Catlin to stage an exhibition of his work at the Institution, and to take up residence in its 'Castle', as the oldest of the Institution's buildings was known.[8]

At this time, Catlin was considering another grand endeavor, which he outlined enthusiastically to Blackmore. This was to consist of two volumes on the Indians, each with one hundred pages of text, and was to be illustrated by almost two hundred photographs.[9] However, this new study was destined never to be produced. In October 1872, in poor health, Catlin took his paintings and left the Smithsonian, and on 23 December he died.

The United States government finally acquired Catlin's paintings in 1879, when Joseph Henry persuaded Harrison's widow to take them out of storage in Philadelphia and donate them to the Smithsonian.

THOMAS MCKENNEY AND CHARLES BIRD KING

At the time that Catlin was beginning his western journeys, another grand endeavor, in this case initially funded by the US government, was well under way. Colonel Thomas L. McKenney (1785–1859), the Superintendent of Indian Trade, and later Commissioner of the Bureau of Indian Affairs, had conceived the idea of a government collection of North American Indian artifacts, to be set up in Washington DC. Like many of his contemporaries, McKenney believed that the native races could only be saved by assimilating them into white culture. He had obtained government support for his 'Archives' ('. . . a collection of items relating to our aborigines preserved there for the inspection of the curious and for the information of future generations and long after the Indians will have been no more'),[10] and hoped to collect '. . . whatever of the aboriginal man can be rescued from the destruction which awaits his race.'[11]

During the winter of 1821–2, the presence in the capital city of the artist Charles Bird King inspired McKenney to add portraits of visiting Indian delegates to this collection.[12] The first of these were made in the following spring, from a large delegation of Pawnee, Oto, Omaha, Kansa and Missouri Indians. King continued to paint visiting Indian delegates for the next twenty years, eventually completing 143 portraits.[13]

McKenney continued to add portraits by King and other artists to the government collection until 1827, when he was officially informed that 'nearly all the likenesses have been collected which it is desirable to obtain.'[14] Cost, however, seems to have been the real factor, as McKenney had spent over $3,100 on paintings which were not easily justifiable as necessities.[15] McKenney tried to defend his actions in documenting the Indians in an open letter, but that did nothing to persuade anti-Indian congressmen, who felt that he had wasted federal funds 'for pictures of those wretches',[16] and in 1830 he was dismissed. Most of King's portraits eventually came to the Smithsonian Institution, where they were placed on exhibit.

Before he left office, McKenney resolved to publish the paintings as hand-colored lithographs in a series of twenty volumes, each of which would contain six portraits. Although neither his dismissal nor production problems stopped him from following this plan, his extraordinary commitment drained both his energy and financial resources. Eventually, Judge James Hall, a wealthy amateur who wished to make his name in the field of Indian studies, came to his aid, and was made a partner in the project. The first volume of McKenney and Hall's *History of the Indian Tribes of North America* was finally published in 1836; the last appeared in 1844, some fifteen years after the project had begun.

McKenney at last became estranged from the work, and Hall complained that because only wealthy patrons or great libraries could afford the high cost of the set of volumes ($120), its limited circulation did not bring him the renown he hoped for. The portraits were, however, authentic, and, as noted by the press, 'one of the largest and most splendid works which the literature and arts of the country have ever produced.'[17]

SETH EASTMAN

Most attempts to record the American Indians were tied to a greater or lesser degree to the government, since it alone could afford to support artists and photographers and publish the results.

Military personnel serving on America's frontier had a unique opportunity to study the Indians. Lieutenant Seth Eastman (1809–75) was a West Point graduate who had been trained as an artist. His first major posting, in 1830, was to Fort Snelling, Minnesota, where soon after his arrival he began to record the local Sioux and Chippewa Indians. In 1833 he returned to West Point to serve as the assistant drawing teacher.[18]

Eastman was finally able to rejoin his Fort Snelling regiment in 1841, when, although this was not yet part of his official duties, he had more time to paint the Indians, and began to establish his reputation. By 1846 he had completed more than four hundred oil paintings and watercolors.[19]

His wife, the author Mary Eastman, was equally interested in recording the lifestyles of the Indians. In their first collaboration, *Dahcotah; or, Life and Legends of the Sioux Around Fort Snelling* (1849), she summed up their work.

'It will still be my endeavor to depict all the customs, feasts and ceremonies of the Sioux, before it be too late . . . They are receding rapidly, and with feeble resistance, before the giant strides of civilization. The hunting grounds of a few savages will soon become the haunts of densely peopled, civilized settlements. We should be better reconciled to this manifest destiny of the aborigines, if the inroads of civilization were worthy of it.'[20]

In 1849, Eastman also began an official collaboration with the US government. By the 1840s, the Congressional antipathies that had put a stop to Thomas McKenney's collecting activities had swung in the other direction. On 4 March 1847, Congress authorized an exhaustive study of American Indian tribes, thus involving the Office of Indian Affairs once again in collecting information and images of the Indians. Henry Rowe Schoolcraft, an ethnologist, agreed to collect information and write the text of the study, and it was hoped that George Catlin would supply the illustrations. When Catlin refused (one must remember that he had his own plans, and that Congress had previously refused to buy his gallery of American Indian paintings), the offer was made to Eastman. Eastman was eager to turn his enthusiasm into a vocation, and in 1850 was transferred to Washington DC to begin work.

During the next five years, Eastman prepared approximately 275 pages of illustrations for the first five volumes of Schoolcraft's *Indian Tribes of the United States*.[21] However, while the government could afford the considerable expenses of publication, it would not agree to pay Eastman a reasonable salary for his work as well, and amid financial problems and disillusionment, he finally left the project. Schoolcraft's work was completed by inferior artists; moreover, against contractual obligations, it used unauthorized copies of Eastman's illustrations. Schoolcraft's scholarship has also since been called into question, but Eastman's illustrations still reveal an extraordinary ethnological knowledge and artistic ability.

JOHN MIX STANLEY

In contrast to the Schoolcraft/Eastman project, the majority of the government's use of artists was in connection with various surveys, affording the artists both official and unofficial time to record the American West. Of particular note is John Mix Stanley, who joined a number of expeditions in the 1840s with the specific intention of making paintings of the Indians. In 1852 Stanley loaned his collection of approximately 150 paintings to the Smithsonian Institution, where they were exhibited in the Gallery of Art alongside the Indian portraits of Charles Bird King.

Like Catlin, Stanley hoped the US government would purchase his work. Unfortunately, as with Catlin, it never did, and on 24 January 1865 a devastating fire destroyed the Gallery of Art and all but a handful of the paintings by both Stanley and King. Duplicate oils plus McKenney and Hall's lithographs existed for some of King's paintings, but Stanley's dreams of making his fortune from his Indian paintings literally went up in smoke. He was never recompensed for his loss.

The fire also signaled the end of expensive, time-consuming attempts to record the American Indians on canvas, as the technology of the painter was surpassed by that of the photographer.

WILLIAM HENRY BLACKMORE

After the tragic fire of 1865, Joseph Henry, the Secretary of the Smithsonian, suggested to the then Commissioner of Indian Affairs, Lewis Bogy, that it was time 'to begin anew . . . a far more authentic and trustworthy collection of likenesses of the principal tribes of the United States. The negatives of these might be preserved and copies supplied at cost to any who might desire them. . . The Indians are passing away so rapidly that but few years remain, within which this can be done and the loss will be irretrievable and so felt when they are gone.'[22]

Henry's appeal to Bogy to finance this endeavor was, however, refused, on the grounds that it was the Smithsonian's financial responsibility. Henry was eventually given financial support by the same friend, William Henry Blackmore, who a few years earlier had persuaded him to bring George Catlin to the musuem.

Blackmore is a shadowy figure, who has remained all but unknown to historians. A wealthy English collector and speculator, he was avidly interested in the American West, especially the Indians. It is due to his foresight and financial support that many important early photographs of the American Indians exist, and while he did not invent the tradition, his documentary projects were significant precursors for later, more famous photographic works.

Blackmore's ideas for a photographic record of the Indians grew slowly. In the same year as the fire at the Smithsonian, the trustees of his museum in Salisbury, England, had published a series of thirty photographic portraits of Indian delegates to Washington DC. These had originally been made by the studio of James Earle McClees during the winter of 1857–8, and represent the first systematic effort to record photographically Indians on a delegation to the capital. With competition from photographic giants such as Jesse Whitehurst and Mathew Brady, it appears that McClees had felt he needed an edge to bring him both attention and business, and had decided that his portraits of the Indians would provide this. However, like artists before and photographers after him, he was also interested in documenting a vanishing race, a point he made clear in his advertising.

'The gallery of portraits includes those of some of the principal Chiefs, Braves, and Councilors [sic] of different tribes. . . Some of them are since dead—killed in battle. To the student of our history, as additions to libraries and historical collections, and as mementoes of the race of red men, now rapidly fading away, this series is of great value and interest. They are executed in the best style of the art, and are confidently presented as exact and characteristic portraits.'[23]

Blackmore had gained access to these negatives through his contact with Antonio Zeno Shindler, a local artist-turned-photographer, who had taken over the management of the McClees studio. Their English publication lists the wrong delegation dates ('1850–1863'), and the McClees studio is not credited, but it was nonetheless a significant event in that it represented Blackmore's first attempt at producing a series of American Indian photographs.

As well as financing his own museum, Blackmore also contributed heavily to the United States Geological Survey of the Territories (under Ferdinand V. Hayden), and to the Smithsonian Institution. He traveled around the United States, commissioning photographers and collecting photographs of the Indians, then allowed Shindler to make copies of this valuable collection for the Smithsonian. Many of these images were shown in the Smithsonian's Gallery of Art in 1867, in its first exhibition of photographs. In 1869 the Museum also published an exhibition list, which was popularly known as the *Shindler Catalogue*, another small step for Blackmore.

In 1868, while traveling with the Hayden survey, Blackmore's thoughts finally came into focus. He obtained several volumes of the world's first major photographic ethnographic study—Watson and Forbes's *The People of India*—and forwarded these to the Smithsonian. Envisioning a similar publication on the American Indians, he promptly proposed such a project to Hayden. It would consist of six to ten volumes, with fifty photographs in each and six to eight photographs for each tribe.[24]

An undertaking such as this would be expensive, and would require the effort of many people. Therefore, in 1870, Blackmore proposed that the Smithsonian should take the work under its wing. The Institution had already benefitted from his activities, and was receptive to the idea, but no specific plans were forthcoming.

For such a publication to become a reality, more images had to be collected, and in 1872 Blackmore contracted Alexander Gardner to photograph visiting Indian delegations. Once again his own museum published the images, in a series of ten albums of over two hundred and forty portraits, representing nineteen tribes. Blackmore was getting closer to his goal.

While the Smithsonian exhibited Blackmore's photographs, the negatives were controlled by Hayden's United States Geological Survey of the Territories. Gardner's 1872 negatives were added to the earlier ones that had been used to make the Smithsonian exhibit. Also under its control were the survey negatives by William Henry Jackson and others.

As Hayden's collection of negatives grew, there was an increasing need to catalog them. In 1874 Jackson himself prepared a list of the Indian photographs, acknowledging the 'munificent liberality' of William Blackmore, 'who has contributed them gratuitously for the advancement of ethnological studies.'[25]

Although Blackmore's publishing venture had still not become a reality, he continued to make plans.[26] A second, expanded catalog was produced by Jackson in 1877, and the introduction again noted Blackmore's importance and his intention 'to enlarge it to include, if possible, all the tribes of the North American continent.'[27] An attempt was made to produce a larger version of this catalog, illustrated with photographs, but as others had found out, the expense was too great, and only a few sets were ever produced. This was, in fact, the closest Blackmore ever came to seeing his planned publication become a reality. Given that similar projects bankrupted photographers such as Mathew Brady and later Edward S. Curtis, Blackmore could be seen as having been spared their financial fate. However, other of his business dealings, including attempts to buy large land holdings in the American West did lead to bankruptcy, and ultimately he committed suicide.

Although Blackmore failed to publish his grand endeavor he did succeed in several smaller ventures, and more importantly, in preserving portraits of American Indians and their lifestyles for future generations. In 1879 Congress consolidated various American surveys into the United States Geological Survey, and the Indian negatives came under the care of the newly created Bureau of Ethnology (later the Bureau of American Ethnology), under the control of the Smithsonian Institution. They are now in the Smithsonian's National Anthropological Archives.

Realistically, dreams of creating an all-encompassing record of the American Indians were almost certain to fail. Those who envisioned such projects may have been unrealistic, or perhaps they did understand the problems but still felt the necessity of turning their dreams into fact. Whatever the cost to themselves, these artists and photographers left an irreplaceable record for later generations of researchers, and created the path for future photographers to follow.

Eagle of Delight, an Oto. Lithograph published by McKenney and Hall from a painting by Charles Bird King, dated 1821. One of the most striking of McKenney and Hall's lithographic portraits, Eagle of Delight was described as 'young, tall, her face . . . was the most beautiful we had met.' In 1821 she traveled with her husband to Washington DC, where she captivated the President and nearly everyone else she met. Soon after King painted her portrait, she returned home and died from measles.

*Keokuk, also known as The
Watchful Fox, of the Sac and
Fox tribe, by George Catlin,
1835. One of the early works in
Catlin's attempt to record 'every
tribe of Indians on the Continent'.
According to Catlin, there was
'. . . no Indian chief on the
frontier better known at this time,
or more highly appreciated for his
eloquence . . . when he was
contending for his people's rights.'
After Catlin had painted his
portrait, Keokuk 'had the vanity
to say . . . that he made a fine
appearance on horseback, and
that he wished me to paint him
thus.'*

*Indian mode of traveling, by
Seth Eastman, 1869. Eastman
used one of his early oil paintings
(now lost) as the basis for this
work. His early paintings were
also used as the basis for
illustrations during his
government-funded collaboration
on Schoolcraft's* Indian Tribes of
the United States.

A heavily retouched photograph of the Smithsonian Institution 'Castle' in flames, 24 January 1865. The fire began when workmen in the Smithsonian, wishing to combat the bitter cold, unknowingly connected their stove to a flue that had been closed. This caused the roof to catch fire, burning down the Gallery of Art and destroying most of the Indian paintings by John Mix Stanley and Charles Bird King.
ALEXANDER GARDNER

Hunting Buffalo, by John Mix Stanley, 1845. One of the very few of Stanley's irreplaceable paintings to survive the fire at the Smithsonian Institution in 1865.

Petalashara, also known as Man and Chief, Pawnee. Taken in Washington DC in 1858, this photograph is one in an elegant series of portraits that were among the earliest attempts to document the American Indians. Studio of James Earle McClees

Independent Master Photographers

T HE PERIOD from the 1890s through to the first decades of the twentieth century were a time of rapid change for the North American Indians. The attractions of the West, especially the Southwest, encouraged many independent photographers to document the 'vanishing races', and in so doing, to create a number of notable photographic masterpieces. Four independent photographers have been selected for detailed study here. Each had a different approach, but all of them chose to live closely with their subjects, an experience that had an impact both on their lives and on their photography.

The first, John Anderson, recorded one Plains Indian group, the Brule Dakota, and experimented with various photographic styles. The second, a team of commercial photographers, Lloyd Winter and Percy Pond, actually became members of a Northwest Coast tribe, and recorded the Indians' changing lifestyle, without resorting to the elimination of Anglo-American cultural elements. The third, George Wharton James, was a driven crusader who championed the traditional lifestyle of the Indians of the Southwest while maintaining that their lives had to change. And lastly Sumner Matteson used a bicycle, a simple Kodak camera and his warm personality to enable him to travel the West and create snapshot masterpieces of the Indians.

JOHN ALVIN ANDERSON

In 1878 the Rosebud Reservation was established in Dakota Territory (now in South Dakota) for the Brule Sioux. Two years later, in 1880, Fort Niobrara was established in Nebraska to protect settlers from the same Indians. Against this backdrop of evolving Indian–White relations, the young John Anderson arrived with his family to begin a lifelong involvement with photography and the Indians.

Anderson was born in Sweden on 25 March 1869, and emigrated with his family to the United States, moving to the area of Fort Niobrara in the mid-1880s. He purchased his first camera out of savings from his wages as a carpenter,[1] and in 1885 was commissioned to act as civilian photographer for the United States Army at the fort, from which date he began recording life on the Rosebud Reservation. Up to this point, Anderson's photography had been more of a sideline than a profession, but in the 1880s he became apprenticed to an important frontier photographer, William R. Cross, who had a studio at Fort Niobrara.[2]

He Dog (1836–1927), a Brule Dakota of the Rosebud Reservation. The photograph probably dates from between 1895 and 1915. This majestic portrait represents the high point of Anderson's photographic career.
JOHN ALVIN ANDERSON

Anderson spent several years working with Cross, but by 1889, when he was serving as the official photographer of the Crook Treaty Commission at the Rosebud Reservation, he was on his own. Taking advantage of his situation, he began recording the daily lives of the Indians, such as the government beef issues. His photographic views at this time are documentary in nature, efficient and accurate, yet although true to their purpose and comparable to other photographers' works on similar subjects, they are largely devoid of artistic vision. However, one should not be too hard on frontier photographers, given the many potential hazards of their pursuit. Donald Hogg, a great-nephew of John Anderson, related how the photographer lost his first camera:

> 'He was preparing to take a picture of a beef issue. The beef was still "on the hoof".
> He had just focused his camera and still had his head under the dark cloth when on
> the ground glass he saw a longhorn steer charging straight for him. The camera was
> demolished. We were lucky to salvage Uncle John.'[3]

Anderson returned to Pennsylvania for the first time in 1890. On one of his repeat trips, in 1895, he married Myrtle Miller. Although he had family and friends in Pennsylvania, the lure of the West and the Indians drew him back, and in 1891 he returned to Nebraska to run Shaw's Art Gallery, a photography studio in the town of Valentine, and to live on the Rosebud Reservation. Since making a full-time living from photography was difficult, Anderson also began working as a clerk at the nearby Jordan's Trading Post.[4]

Throughout his career, Anderson experimented with varying styles for varying types of photography, ranging from strictly documentary images for contract and commercial purposes, to overly romantic, 'nostalgic' re-creations of Indian life. This ability to bridge different styles sets him apart from other photographers. Anderson developed close personal relationships with the Indians, and emerges as one of the all-time master portrait photographers of the American Indian.

Living on the reservation brought Anderson close to the Indians on a daily basis, and many of his subjects became his friends. It is this period of time that represents the true beginning of his photographic involvement with the Brule.

Alma Carlson Roosa, Anderson's niece, recalled that 'At first they [the Indians] resented having their pictures taken, but later they gave him that privilege when they found he was honest with them.' She added 'We never feared the Sioux perhaps because Uncle John was so friendly with them.'[5]

John Anderson's compassion for the Indians was also recorded by one of his employees, Charley Eads, who noted 'I've seen hungry old Indians with no money come in and go back and talk with John, and he would give them things to take home and eat, and then charge them to himself.'[6]

In fact, the entire Anderson family was involved with the Indians in a positive way. Myrtle did many charitable things for the Indian women ('They loved her and she loved them,' Alma Roosa said),[7] and John's brother, Charles, helped to build houses for the Indians on the reservation.[8]

For the most part, Anderson captured his feelings with a camera and not a pen, but in 1896 he produced a small photographic booklet entitled *Among the Sioux*. By this time he had already witnessed many changes to the lives of the Indians, which he had initially viewed as progress. In his introduction, he wrote 'In presenting this brochure to the public, I would ask its acceptance on the ground that the manners, customs, home-life, progress and development herein portrayed are both accurate and reliable and that they represent, in brief, a phase of life little known by the public at large.'[9]

In 1900, Anderson's photography reached an artistic high point. He produced a series of magnificent portraits of He Dog, Turning Bear, Fool Bull, Good Voice and One Star, among others, revealing the dignity of these individuals, who were also his friends.

By 1911, Anderson's work had taken on another dimension. Perhaps struck by the rapidly accelerating cultural changes he saw around him, his work began to emphasize the old, traditional ways of Indian life over the so-called progressive elements. The 'vanishing races' had become a personal reality, and while Anderson saw change as good, he now felt the necessity of recording life as it was. With the help of the Indians themselves, he re-created scenes from their daily lives, such as traditional methods of dressing hides or cooking, as accurately as possible, without didactic or romantic overtones.

In February 1922, after a big farewell party given by the Brule, the Andersons moved to California for health reasons. Once again, however, the lure of the Indians was too strong, and by October they had returned to Rosebud.

In 1925 the Andersons suffered a tragic loss with the death of their only son, Roscoe. That same year they began to encourage and provide financial support for a young Brule boy by the name of Ben Reifel (see illustration overleaf). Under their encouragement, he completed high school in three years, earned masters and doctoral degrees from Harvard and was ultimately elected to the House of Representatives.[10] Personal involvement of this magnitude marked not only Anderson's life, but influenced almost half a century of his photography.

Disaster struck again in 1928, when, only three years after the loss of their son, the Andersons' home burnt down, destroying most of John's negatives. Fortunately, those for his greatest masterpieces were spared.[11]

Ben Reifel, circa 1925. Reifel was the young Brule boy who received encouragement and financial support from the Andersons after the death of their only son in 1925, and who was eventually elected to the United States House of Representatives.
JOHN ALVIN ANDERSON

Sioux Memory Gems was published by Anderson in 1929, and consisted of a collection of poems written by his wife and illustrated with his photographs. These images were clearly staged, and by today's standards are overly romantic. The style is, however, commensurate with the purpose of the book, and perhaps understandably nostalgic, given the changes in the Andersons' own lives as well as in those of the Indians.

During the 1930s the Andersons moved first to Rapid City, South Dakota, to manage the Sioux Indian Museum (built to house their personal ethnographic collection), then back to their home in California. Stained-glass memorial windows in the Trinity Episcopal Church

on the Rosebud Reservation honor not only the memory of John Anderson, who died in 1948, but also his wife and son.[12]

Numerous other photographers lived with specific Indian groups and, like John Anderson, they changed and were changed in turn by their contact with the Indians. It takes a master to assimilate these opportunities, but it takes a humanist, touched by the lives of those around him, to become a master of Anderson's sensitivity. Anderson maximized his wide-ranging opportunities and artistic abilities, and this allowed his photography to evolve from the documentary to the regal.

WINTER AND POND

While John Anderson was photographing the Brule, Lloyd Winter and Percy Pond, far to the north-west in Alaska, were unwittingly watching a dance that would change both their lives and photographic careers.

'One evening they were sitting on the side of a hill when a group of brightly dressed Indians appeared on the grassy knoll beneath them. They formed into a line, then a circle, chanting a song. One at a time they would enter the circle and perform a dance. The Indians were changing happily when they spotted Lloyd and Percy; then they all began talking excitedly together. Finally, one of the Indians climbed the hill to where Lloyd and Percy sat. Luckily Lloyd understood his language, which was Chilkat, and the man told him that their dances were a Chilkat secret and that no one else was ever to see them. They had thought of a way around the disaster of two white men observing the dances, however, by offering them membership in the Chilkat tribe. So that day they both became Chilkat chiefs—with names. Percy was to be called Kitch-ka (Crow Man), and Lloyd, Kinda (Winter).'[13]

This incident occurred in 1894, and contributed greatly to Winter and Pond's success in recording the Tlingit and Haida Indians of Alaska.

The year before, at the age of twenty-seven, Lloyd Winter had traveled from California to Juneau, Alaska, to explore the gold-mining possibilities. Once there he met George M. Landerking, a local photographer, who invited Winter to join his business. Within a few months, Winter had been joined by a friend from California, Percy Pond, and in July they bought the studio, reopening it under their own names. Together they operated the studio until Pond's death in 1943.[14]

Lloyd Winter was, by training, a portrait painter, and had studied at the California School of Design. This training no doubt helped him to compose artistic portraits and scenic views. But to obtain intimate images of the Indians, he needed more than an artist's background—like John Anderson, he needed to develop long-term, friendly relationships with his subjects.

Many photographers, both professional and amateur, traveled to Alaska, especially after the advent of the Kodak camera and the Klondike gold rush of 1898. Most tourists visited the area in summer, when the Indians were away from their winter villages, being engaged in fishing, mining and other summer activities elsewhere. As a result, these photographers recorded static views of empty villages, totem poles and the like. The work of Winter and Pond is significantly different because as yearlong residents with a genuine interest in the local cultures, they developed lasting friendships which gave them access to situations beyond those caught by the transient summer photographers.[15]

Although they both spoke the native Chilkat language, Winter and Pond still found the Indians sometimes unwilling to allow their photographs to be taken. William Jorgenson, a friend of Winter and Pond, recounted this reluctance:

Tlingit village of Klukwan on the Chilkat River, Alaska, probably in the spring of 1895.
WINTER AND POND

'I know now that much of what Winter was able to take was strictly on the basis of his personal relationship with these people—the fact that he had been adopted by them. I recall very well his telling me that he still had to be extremely careful. His method was to tell them that he would like to photograph them, and maybe a week later, maybe a year later, they would come into the store and tell him they were ready.' [16]

Even though the Indians were sometimes hesitant, their trust in Winter and Pond is evident by the fact that the photographers were invited to attend and photograph ceremonial events such as the potlatches that commemorated important events in an Indian's life—for example a marriage, house dedication or assumption of a position of leadership. Aside from being 'closed' occasions in isolated regions, potlatches had been suppressed by the white authorities, and documentary evidence of their continuation could have created great problems for the Indians. No photographer could possibly have obtained images of these ceremonies without the knowledge, consent and trust of the participants.

Some of Winter and Pond's most striking images were taken in the winter of 1894–5, and include views of the Whale House at Klukwan, then under the care of a clan leader, George Shotridge. They recorded its magnificent interior (technically a difficult endeavor, given the lighting problems of the day), and at the same time photographed dancers posed outdoors in ceremonial regalia.

It is obvious that Winter and Pond were not trying to re-create an Indian past unaffected by European culture, nor did they produce romantically perfect images of individuals. Instead they documented the Indians around them as they appeared, both prosperous and poor, wearing clothing influenced by several cultures. They could easily have supplied costume props, but a comparison of the clothing in their portraits discounts such a practice.

COPYRIGHT BY WINTER & POND.

For one reason or another, however, some of the portraits show ethnographically inconsistent elements, suggesting that some staging had occurred.[17] As evidenced by Winter and Pond's inadvertent observation of a private ceremony, non-initiates were forbidden to view certain activities, and photography would be the ultimate violation. Thus it is reasonable to assume that the Indians were unwilling to be recorded in the 'correct' attire for certain ceremonies, in order that no secrets would be revealed to the uninitiated. Initiates would know the difference, while non-initiates could still buy exotic photographs without obtaining privileged information. Nonetheless, Winter and Pond's strikingly beautiful photographs contain a wealth of information about the changing native cultures in Alaska.

Although most of their Indian photography dates from the decades around the turn of the century, Winter and Pond continued to have a deep personal interest in the Indians throughout their lives, and in 1928 Winter applied for membership of the Alaska Native Brotherhood, an all-Indian organization. He was accepted as he was able to give as references the six Chilkat men who had adopted him thirty-four years before.[18]

The Alaska Native Brotherhood had been founded by native Indians under the aegis of the Presbyterian church. Their objectives were 'to assist and encourage the Native in his advancement from his native state to his place among the cultivated races of the world, to oppose, discourage, and overcome the narrow injustice of race prejudice, and to aid in the development of the Territory of Alaska.'[19] The organization was seeking citizenship and equal rights for natives, and for control of their lives to be placed in their own hands, not the government's.[20] That Winter was allowed to join is testament to the Indians' trust in him.

Percy Pond died on 1 June 1943, at the age of 71; Lloyd Winter on 18 November 1945. Six Indians served as Winter's honorary pallbearers.[21] The studio continued to operate under a former assistant until it closed in 1956, an event that made front-page news in the *Juneau Independent*.[22]

It would be wrong to assume that Winter and Pond photographed only the Alaskan Indians, or that they had any systematic plan to document Indian culture. Indeed, Indian subjects account for perhaps 400 of their negatives out of a total of 4,700.[23] Nonetheless, they did produce an unparalleled artistic record of the Northwest Coast Indians, resulting from their close personal relationships with and knowledge of their subjects. Their legacy lives on in their photographs.

GEORGE WHARTON JAMES

While Winter and Pond found access to Northwest Coast Indian ceremonies extremely difficult for photographers, George Wharton James complained that there were so many photographers vying for views of the Hopi Snake dance (a dramatized prayer for rain which lasted sixteen days and attracted hordes of tourists) that they were 'kicking down another fellow's tripod and sticking his elbow in the next fellow's lens,' and half-a-dozen or more Indian policemen were needed to keep them in line.[24] Eventually the Hopi banned photographers from attending their dances.

Winter and Pond had approached the Indians in a spirit of friendship. By contrast, James set about photographing the Indians of the Southwest with the unrepenting zeal of a crusader, who stopped at nothing to obtain the views he desired.

James was born in Gainsborough, near Lincoln, England, on 27 September 1858, the same year that James E. McClees produced his early photographs of the Indian delegation to Washington DC. As a youth he suffered from asthma, which restricted his activities and encouraged him to be studious. By the age of sixteen, he had taken up writing and was active in the local Methodist church, preaching and teaching Sunday school.[25] In 1880 he married, and in 1881, hoping to relieve his health problems, he emigrated to the United States and settled in Nevada. He was ordained, and through his early work as an itinerant preacher in Nevada and California, made his first contacts with American Indians, the Paiute and Washo.

In 1887 James moved his family to California, where he came into contact with the Indians of the Franciscan missions. Through these early encounters, he was able to witness at first hand the dramatic changes caused by the impact of 'civilization' on the lives of the Indians. In 1889 James's own life would change dramatically, when his wife accused him of 'remarkable feats of adultery' and assorted other charges.[26] He was defrocked, and though later exonerated, his career was in ruins.

James fled to the desert to recover.

'It was here that I came . . . broken in health and spirit, and gained the renewing impulse and courage that ultimately won for me a fuller enjoyment of life than I had ever had before . . . There, often weeks at a time, I saw no one but Indians . . . There I regained poise and that outlook on life that has ultimately brought peace, serenity and joy . . . here my real spiritual birth occurred.'[27]

In the desert, James met William Wallace Bass, who owned and operated a camp in the Grand Canyon. Bass persuaded James to travel with him to the nearly inaccessible area where the Havasupai Indians lived. This was an experience that had a deep effect on James. The Havasupai seemed to live a perfect life, in harmony with nature, untouched by the problems of civilization.

Although the desert had been healing, James also went to Chicago to cure his depression, but the overcrowded, vice- and disease-ridden city convinced him that man's degradation was connected to industrialization. James became a believer in Social Darwinism, furthering his belief that social salvation lay in the Southwest, with the Indians.[28] Whereas he had been a preacher, James now became a crusader. For the rest of his life he supported movements ranging from vegetarianism and nude sunbathing to Indian rights, prohibition, women's suffrage and pacifism, and lobbied against vivisection and capital punishment.

In 1892 James moved back to California, to Pasadena. He now had many opportunities to explore, describe and photograph the wonders of the Grand Canyon and the Indians of the region. He also came into contact with the Mission Indians, who had lost their land and livelihoods as the missions were secularized. Defending these Indians and helping them with their problems became one of James's major occupations.[29]

Pasadena was also a mecca for photographers. It attracted such noteworthy artists as Adam Clark Vroman, Charles Fletcher Lummis and Frederick Monsen. It is likely that James either learned photography at this time, or at the very least honed his skills.

The Pasadena photographers, many of whom were members of the Pasadena Camera Club, traveled together on photographic excursions, taking advantage of 'photo opportunities' such as the Hopi Snake dances. They produced, in their own right, masterpieces of American Indian photography. No doubt James knew most, if not all, of these men. He certainly knew Lummis, another crusader-photographer who with due cause accused James of plagiarism in an article entitled 'Untruthful James'; and crossed paths with Vroman, who reprimanded him for invading a sacred Hopi kiva (an underground room used for ceremonies or councils) unannounced and uninvited.[30]

James was obviously working with his own objectives in mind—a mission to record the Indians of the Southwest at all costs. With notepad and camera in tow, he made frequent visits to the Hopi, Navaho, Walapai and Zuni Indians, living with them in order to learn about their lives. Like many other photographers of the time, his goal, backed by his

Hopi Snake dancers passing the entrance to a kiva. James was reprimanded for invading such a sacred place, uninvited. Oraibi pueblo, Arizona, 1898.
GEORGE WHARTON JAMES

experiences, was 'To gather together all that we possibly can of [the Indian's] mode of thought and life, his social and tribal customs, religions, ceremonies, dances, and legends ere it is too late'.[31] James's illustrated lectures touched on all aspects of life in the Southwest, but carried an underlying theme of the Indian's tragic situation.

It is known that James sometimes took professional photographers, such as C. C. Pierce and Frederick H. Maude along with him, and that he did not always use his own photographs to illustrate his publications. However, even a cursory look at the images James chose to copyright shows a master photographer at work.

Known to the Hopi as 'Black Bear' because of his full beard,[32] James first photographed their Snake dance in 1896. As an amateur anthropologist he became interested in the ceremony, and was dissatisfied with accounts that described it only as a 'wild, chaotic, yelling, shouting, pagan dance.' In 1898 he published an illustrated booklet, *The Mokis and Their Snake Dance*. This year proved to be a high point in his photographic career, as evinced by the artistic quality of his views.

James wrote many books extolling the beauty of the Southwest, and firmly believed that the evils of the Industrial Age could be countered if Indian virtues were adopted by the white man. Although he did not think of the Indians as his cultural equals, almost everything about Hopi life impressed James. Their ability to survive the hardships imposed by their environment made them strong and taught them to live a simple, natural, and therefore healthy life.[33] As with his other causes, James made his crusade known to the public, summing up his feelings in one of his most popular lectures, later published as a book: *What the White Man May Learn from the Indian*.

'Of course it is not true that all Indians are good Indians, but it is fiendish to believe that the only good Indians are dead Indians. This legend of the whites has done incalculable harm. There are noble Indians, such as Fenimore Cooper described. His pictures are true to the soul of most Indians. The Indian needs what is good in our civilization, and we should not forget that there are many things he can teach us . . . He is the splendid, noble, original American, worthy of citizenship, with his heart open to the truth of Christianity, a ward of the Nation to be protected and not abused.'[34]

Even though James felt that the Indians had much to teach the industrialized world, he still forsaw that eventually their lives must change.

'In simple cunning the . . . Indian may be our superior, but . . . His bow and arrow tipped with obsidian or flint opposed to our Gatling guns; his mule and burro against our iron horse . . . all demonstrate him to be . . . at an intellectual disadvantage. He makes a fine figure in our romances, but I sadly fear that the knell of his doom has sounded, and that a few generations hence he will be no more.'[35]

James's popularity grew as his dynamic personality enthralled readers and audiences alike. His ends, as always, justified his means, and he was persistent in his attempts to gain whatever he wanted (for example, he had thought nothing of going into the sacred Hopi kiva). He cared little for the feelings of those he photographed, although there were times when even his persistence did not pay off. Once he encountered resistance while trying to photograph a 'Yuma Apache' (Western Yavapai) girl, who had gone to school and spoke English, but preferred to live a more traditional lifestyle. Even though James tried every trick in the book, his plans were thwarted.

'To photograph her was impossible. She was determined not to allow anyone to make a picture of her . . . and to gain the picture surreptitiously was equally impossible. She knew every wile of the photographer. There was no opportunity given to place the camera accidentally in position and get a snap when she was not expecting it.'

But he continued his story:

'The Apaches [Western Yavapai] are very averse to being pictured, and all who knew them prophesied that my visit photographically would be without results. The accompanying engravings are but a small quota of those I succeeded in obtaining.'[36]

Blinded perhaps by his goals, James obviously let nothing get in his way. While he may be condemned for his extreme actions, we must not forget that he was driven by deep inner beliefs that led him to champion successfully many Indian causes. His photographic masterpieces were not conceived as mere commercial enterprises, nor as straight documentation of a changing culture. James used his photographs to extoll the virtues of traditional Indian life, and, more importantly, to further Indian rights. As Theodore Roosevelt remarked 'He has done more to make the wonders of the Southwest known to the world than any other ten men.'[37]

By the time of his death in 1923, James had written over forty books, scores of major pamphlets and hundreds of newspaper and magazine articles. Explorer, amateur ethnologist and master photographer, James approached life as he approached photography, with 'a passionate ardour and tireless perseverance',[38] and his photographs are now important documents of American Indian life.

SUMNER W. MATTESON

Sumner W. Matteson, Jr. had as much zeal for adventure as George Wharton James had for crusading. Like James, Matteson distinguished himself photographically with his work on the Indians of the Southwest, especially the Hopi, but while James had concentrated on this region, Matteson extended his range, roaming around most of the western United States on his bicycle. From 1898 to 1908 Matteson traveled more than 25,000 miles and took almost 12,000 photographs recording various aspects of life in the Wild West,[39] including the Indians, wild horse round-ups, salmon fishing and the San Francisco earthquake, together with occasional light-hearted self-portraits, made along the way.

Like thousands of others, Matteson had been caught up in the craze for photography that swept America in the 1890s. Before this date, photography had largely been the domain of professionals, due to its complicated procedures and heavy equipment, but Kodak's new easy-to-use camera and roll film, plus the company's catchphrase—'You press the button, we do the rest'—persuaded people of all ages to take up the craft. Matteson's introduction to it was probably more a coincidence than a conscious career move—the attraction of an interesting activity to an adventurous spirit.

In 1888 Matteson received his Bachelor of Science degree from the University of Minnesota at Minneapolis,[40] where he had been a member of the Chi Psi fraternity, an organization whose address he would use later in life as a base for some of his photographic activities. In 1895 he began selling Victor bicycles for the Overman Wheel Company in St Paul, Minnesota. By the following year, he had become the manager of the company in Denver, Colorado. Overmans also sold Kodak cameras, in a portable case which could be clamped to a bicycle. The combination was perfect and within no time at all, Matteson was hooked.

Matteson's first photographic forays recorded activities such as bicycle excursions and hunting trips around Colorado, and were used in an advertising campaign called 'Colorado Snaps', for which new negatives were 'added at the slightest provocation.'[41] Matteson's free spirit soon got the better of him, and he set off to seek adventure, if not fortune, and unwittingly to produce his own unique photographic record of the American Indians.

By 1900 Matteson was listed in the Denver City Directory as a Traveling Correspondent. Perhaps a better description would have been 'Photojournalist' or 'Essayist', as he had a habit of documenting activities sequentially as well as recording peripheral events. Within a year, he was selling his views for use in magazines and other publications.

Although Matteson had photographed the Canyon de Chelly and Chaco Canyon in Arizona and New Mexico, the true beginning of his Indian photography was in 1900, when he again traveled to the Southwest. Joining the ranks of hundreds of tourists and photographers, he recorded the Hopi Snake and Flute dances, and as James had also discovered, was not alone in his attempts. Given the number of photographers recording the dances, it is not surprising that Matteson's handy little Kodak also recorded another master, Adam Clark Vroman, at work.

Perhaps because it was an early attempt, Matteson was never quite happy with his Flute ceremony series. He always wanted to redo it 'as I think it never has been done scientifically.' [42] However, his 'Moki [Hopi] Madonna' won a $60 prize from the Eastman Kodak Company.[43] In addition, Burton Holmes, a famous travel writer, used fifty-six of Matteson's Hopi photographs and only thirty by Vroman to illustrate one of his essays.[44]

Matteson's abilities as a photographer were soon noticed, and in 1901 he returned to the Southwest as a backup photographer for a Field Columbian Museum Expedition. He recorded every phase of the Hopi Snake and Antelope ceremonies over a nine-day period, as well as taking shots of everyday life in the pueblos. He had the misfortune to lose about half of his best Hopi negatives, due to a pinhole leak in his bellows,[45] but was at least more fortunate than another photographer, George Ben Wittick, who died from a snakebite.[46]

In 1902 Matteson took a job with William Henry Jackson's Photochrom Company, accompanying the legendary photographer throughout the West.[47] Perhaps because the company did not give credit to individual photographers, or because Matteson preferred to be an independent free spirit, he soon left Photochrom and began photographing the Great Plains and entertaining audiences with his illustrated lectures of life in the American West.

In 1905 or 1906 Matteson created his second significant series of Indian photographs, when he recorded the Sun dance of the Gros Ventre and Assiniboin Indians at Fort Belknap, Montana. One of the changes wrought upon the Indians by reservation life was that they were no longer free to hold their ceremonies when they wanted, and Matteson's article in the *Pacific Monthly* described the events surrounding what was probably the last Sun dance. One Major Logan, who was in charge of the reservation, was willing 'to let the Indians plan their own entertainment, as long as they respected reservation rules, and it was the Indian's wish to live over as far as possible scenes of the times when the beloved buffalo stood upon their land'.[48] Matteson's description of the dances captures both the beauty and the poignancy of the occasion.

> 'The dances were the occasion for the display of such an array of bare skin, buckskin, paint, quills, beads, shells, teeth, feathers and weasel skins as I never hope to see again . . . The Participants were for the most part men past middle age, who had gone through many a real encounter, and who took a pardonable pride in living over the scenes that revealed their cunning and skill.'[49]

Tuesday was the day of the Fool dance, in which participants clothed themselves in coarse cloth, painted their faces grotesquely, and fastened great slabs of raw meat wherever it would hold. Suddenly one or two would turn on the crowd and hurl a piece of meat at the nearest horse or human being. Matteson could not resist.

'Here was something out of the ordinary in the way of photographs, so I lost no time in breaking through the circle of spectators. This ambitious step on my part was taken as a challenge, and immediately I became the target for the bloody missiles. It was no small task to dodge several assailants at a time and to save my camera as well, but I stood my ground.'[50]

Wednesday was the highlight of the week, and consisted of the building of the Medicine Lodge and the Sun dance. Matteson carefully recorded the stage by stage building of the lodge and the dance, in photographic sequences that combine ethnographic documentation with artistic mastery, representing the culmination of all his Indian photography. A descendant of one of the men photographed that day commented:

'The manner in which the Indian people are portrayed in these photographs is unique, for Sumner Matteson seems to have had a rare ability to gain the confidence and trust of a people in a very short time. Perhaps they sensed his free spirit, something they no longer possessed. At any rate, he was allowed to enter and photograph ceremonies and events that were previously forbidden to outsiders . . . It could be that the Indian people realized . . . that their way was fading away and they wanted a record of these activities.'[51]

Matteson continued to travel around the country taking photographs. In 1908 he hoped to travel with the US fleet for *Collier's* magazine, but was not hired as he had not made his reputation as a writer. Although he accepted this turn of events with a positive attitude ('I am better off here than trying to develop films in the hot water of the tropics and wearing a dress suit at the same time. In fact, I am a better Indian than Diplomat'),[52] it is possible that for Matteson himself, this signaled the end of his ten-year adventure. Even though President Theodore Roosevelt considered his photographs 'corkers',[53] only nine months later Matteson would write 'I have given up the chase for a while and do not expect to make any more negatives this winter.'[54] Indeed, he settled down in Milwaukee as a book-keeper for the Milwaukee Coke and Gas Company, and virtually gave up photography.[55] He made one final trip in 1920, when he journeyed to Mexico. On 26 October, after climbing Mount Popocatapétl and staying too long, his lungs froze and he died.

The legacy of Sumner Matteson lives on. In 1976, the Sumner W. Matteson, Jr. Native American Scholarship was established for students of the Fort Belknap Reservation in Montana. An essential qualification is a deep and lasting interest in tribal traditions and the welfare of the people.[56]

George Horse Capture, a descendant of one of the Gros Ventre Indians photographed by Matteson, provides the best insight into his work and that of other master photographers of the American Indian:

'These materials irrefutably prove that we are of this place. These are our people, and we are a great people; we possess strengths previously unknown. We are thankful that our images have been recorded so vividly.'[57]

RIGHT
Katie Blue Thunder, a Brule Dakota, born in 1892 and photographed here in 1900.
JOHN ALVIN ANDERSON

FAR RIGHT
Yellow Hair (1835–1913) of the Brule Dakota, and a woman, probably his wife, photographed in 1900.
JOHN ALVIN ANDERSON

YELLOW-HAIR & WIFE
COPYRIGHT 1900.
BY J.A.ANDERSON

LEFT

Sam Kills Two, a Brule Dakota, painting a winter count in 1926. Some Plains tribes kept records of events by means of symbolic figures or pictographs, but we do not know if Sam Kills Two's winter count was an original, or one produced for the photograph.

JOHN ALVIN ANDERSON

ABOVE

Fool Bull (1844–1909), a Brule Dakota, photographed in 1900.

JOHN ALVIN ANDERSON

Turning Bear (1848–1911), a Brule Dakota, photographed in 1900.
JOHN ALVIN ANDERSON

Good Voice, a Brule Dakota, circa 1900. The portrait demonstrates that the subjects of these photographs did not need to be wearing traditional dress for the works to be masterpieces.

JOHN ALVIN ANDERSON

One Star, a Brule Dakota, in 1900. JOHN ALVIN ANDERSON

Undated study of an unidentified Brule Dakota woman and child. JOHN ALVIN ANDERSON

*Guests arriving by canoe for a
potlatch dance on the Chilkat
River, Alaska, in 1895. An
example of the private ceremonies
to which the photographers'
initiation into the Tlingit tribe in
1894 enabled them to gain access.*
WINTER AND POND

51

Unidentified woman and child. The photographers' active studio in Juneau, Alaska, catered to Indians and non-Indians alike. It is possible that this undated portrait was taken for the woman, and not for commercial reasons, but many of their photographs record Indians wearing clothing influenced by cultures other than their own.
WINTER AND POND

'Chilkat Indians in Old Dancing Costumes, Alaska'
Various ethnographically inconsistent elements can sometimes be seen in ceremonial photographs. It is possible that the Indians were unwilling to be photographed in their 'correct' ceremonial attire, in order that no secrets should be revealed to the uninitiated.
WINTER AND POND

IXTERIOR OF CHIEF'S HOUSE.   CHILKAT INDIANS IN OLD DANCING COSTUMES. ALASKA   COPYRIGHT BY WINTER & POND.

Interior of the Whale House at Klukwan, 1895. The problems of lighting this shot, with its magnificent examples of Northwest Coast art, were probably solved by combining a long time exposure with natural light, and the possible use of flash powder. The standing man is probably the Chilkat chief, Coudahwot.
WINTER AND POND

206 INDIAN DANCERS AT POTLATCH. CHILKAT

ABOVE
*Chilkat dancers at a potlatch in
Klukwan during the winter of
1894–5.*
WINTER AND POND

ABOVE RIGHT
*Chilkat Chiefs in dancing costumes, 1895. On the left is Coudahwot; on the
right, Yeilgoozu, also known as George Shotridge, the hereditary caretaker of
the Whale House at Klukwan, whose interior is shown on the previous page.*
WINTER AND POND

BELOW RIGHT
'Indian Dancers, Chilkat, Alaska'
WINTER AND POND

LEFT
Tlingit women at Fort Wrangel, Alaska. The subjects of these photographs include both the prosperous and the poor, documented simply as they were.
WINTER AND POND

RIGHT
Undated studio portrait of two native girls, Juneau, Alaska.
WINTER AND POND

Hopi ('Moki') family at Oraibi
pueblo, Arizona, 1898.
GEORGE WHARTON JAMES

RIGHT
Hopi weaver, 1898.
GEORGE WHARTON JAMES

RIGHT
Hopi maiden, matron and child,
1898.
GEORGE WHARTON JAMES

BELOW
'Street in Oraibi, Moki', probably
1898.
GEORGE WHARTON JAMES

COPYRIGHT, 1898, Photo

C. WHARTON JAMES PASADENA, Cal.

1898. SNAKE PRIESTS AT SONG AND PRAYER BEFORE THE KISI.

ABOVE
Hopi Snake dance at Oraibi pueblo, Arizona,
1898. James first photographed the Snake dance
in 1896, having become dissatisfied with
accounts of it by others that described it only as
a 'wild, chaotic, yelling, shouting, pagan dance.'
GEORGE WHARTON JAMES

MOKI SNAKE DANCE, WALPI, 1897 "TAKING THE EMETIC."

G. WHARTON JAMES Photo
PASADENA, CAL.

Hopi Snake dance at Walpi pueblo, Arizona. Several other photographers can be seen in this photograph. James was to complain bitterly of the difficulties he encountered in trying to take photographs on such an occasion.
GEORGE WHARTON JAMES

'A Chemehuevi repairing a baby carrier'
These photographic masterpieces were not
conceived as mere commercial enterprises,
nor as straight documentation of a
changing culture. Instead they were to
extoll the virtues of traditional Indian life,
and to further Indian rights.
COPYRIGHTED BY GEORGE WHARTON JAMES

COPYRIGHT, 1898, G. WHARTON JAMES, PHOTO, PASADENA CAL.

Navaho chiefs inside a hogan (a wooden dwelling covered with earth), 1892.
GEORGE WHARTON JAMES

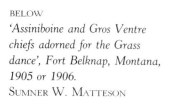

'Assiniboine and Gros Ventre
chiefs adorned for the Grass
dance', Fort Belknap, Montana,
1905 or 1906.
SUMNER W. MATTESON

ABOVE
'Indian matron at age ninety-six',
Fort Belknap, Montana, 1905 or
1906. Cycling around the country
with his Kodak camera, Matteson
produced an invaluable record of
American Indian life.
SUMNER W. MATTESON

RIGHT
Assiniboin/Gros Ventre Fool
dancer resting. Fort Belknap,
Montana, 1905 or 1906.
SUMNER W. MATTESON

'Chief of the Fool Dancers', photographed at Fort Belknap, Montana, 1905 or 1906.
SUMNER
W. MATTESON

*Woman hanging meat to dry
outside a tipi at Fort Belknap,
Montana, 1905 or 1906.*
SUMNER W. MATTESON

ABOVE

Hopi Snake dance, 21 August 1900. The snakes were entrusted with prayers, then released in four directions to carry their messages to the spirits.
SUMNER W. MATTESON

RIGHT

'Old blind man at Oraibi, Arizona', August 1900. This image of a Hopi man is an eloquent example of the photographer's ability to gain the trust of his subjects.
SUMNER W. MATTESON

BELOW
'Praying with snake in spring at
Mishongnovi', August 1901. This
rite was a part of the Hopi Flute
ceremony, which was performed
on alternate years to the Snake
dance, in order to help crops
mature and bring rain.
SUMNER W. MATTESON

ABOVE
'Sunrise procession of Flute ceremony at
Walpi, Arizona', August 1900.
SUMNER W. MATTESON

RIGHT
'Hopi belle at her window, Second Mesa, Arizona',
1901. Although he only used a Kodak camera to
make 'snapshots', the photographer's abilities
and sense of composition enabled him to produce
elegant images, far above the usual standard.
SUMNER W. MATTESON

The Medicine Mo...
Copyright
Gerhard
St...

Expositions and World Fairs

EXPOSITIONS and world fairs serve as showcases for a nation's view of the overall progress it has made from the beginning of its formation to a certain point in its history. They provide an occasion upon which to reflect on the past glories and future prospects of a civilization. Expositions are organized under their respective governments by that country's leading intellectuals, while heads of state—royalty, presidents and even dictators—serve as sponsors. Governments, business communities and private benefactors pay the bills. Participants and visitors alike experience a unique historic event which entertains but also teaches. Expositions are golden opportunities to see the diversity of mankind, to become aware of the differences of our cultures and to understand the universals that we share.

As the conflicts with the North American Indians in the West subsided, various tribes participated in expositions and world fairs as 'living exhibitions'. Chiefs, old warriors, medicine men, artisans, entertainers and families traveled from their homes to the exposition sites, where they re-created their traditional life as part of America's history.

Amateur and professional photographers took pictures of them, and newspapermen and anthropologists wrote about them. We know many of their names and tribes, and we usually know when and from where they came. But, because of the silent voice of the American Indian in our history books, we know very little of why they came, how they felt there, and what it was like when they returned to the reservations.

The expositions offered a unique photographic opportunity. Never before had there been so many Indian people in one place at one time, to be photographed in a peaceful situation. In the past, photographers had to entreat Indians to come into their studios to have their pictures taken, and obtaining images of life on the reservations was even more difficult. It usually took many years of gaining the Indians' trust, plus some fortuitous, unusual circumstance, for a photographer to get access. Moreover, photographing the Indian tribes, whatever their situation, in the American West of the nineteenth century always meant the photographers had to make long and difficult journeys, usually at their own expense.

For the official photographers hired by government commissioners to take photographs at the expositions, most of their costs were paid. For them, and for the studio photographers who also photogaphed the Indians, there were profits to be made. Some published prints in

Shunkapaug, a medicine man, photographed at the Louisiana Purchase Exposition, St Louis, Missouri, in 1904.
GERHARD SISTERS

exposition guides or records, and received publicity for them, and as governments could not hold copyrights, most kept their negatives and could make further prints for future sales.

Although much of the motivation behind becoming an exposition photographer must have been commercial, many of these photographers understood the value of the pictures they were making as documentation of a vanishing race. Some written accounts of their experiences at the expositions have survived, and convey the interplay between the 'shadow catchers' and their subjects. Mostly a shy people from isolated reservations, the Indians became dynamic players on the stage the expositions offered them, and they and the photographers must have been greatly changed by the experience.

EARLY EXPOSITIONS

The era of international expositions began with the opening of the World's Fair at the Crystal Palace in London in May 1851, with Queen Victoria and her consort, Prince Albert, presiding. In his dedication speech, the Prince stated that 'The Exhibition of 1851 is to give us a true text and a living picture of the point of development at which the whole of mankind has arrived.' The public were enthralled, and over six million people visited the exhibition during the course of its run. There were 499 exhibition stands, including eleven ethnographic models. Apart from being excellent works of art, the models served to convey a vivid representation of the customs of natives of distant countries, something which could not be so easily apprehended from drawings or descriptions. There were models of Hindu castes, Thuggee murderers, a Spanish bullfight, Mexican–Indian traders, and the Knights of Malta. The model from America displayed an Indian scalping a white man, which was the popular 'savage' stereotyped viewpoint of the public at the time. Two living Iowa Indians appeared at the Fair to represent the peaceful tribes. Unfortunately, no photographs seem to have been taken of them.[1]

PRINCE ROLAND BONAPARTE

The first expositions at which the ethnic groups in attendance were photographed were sponsored by the French. Prince Roland Bonaparte, grand-nephew of Emperor Napoleon I of France, was one of the first ethnologists to have photographs of American Indians made at European expositions, and fully recognized the value of these images for cross-cultural communications.

Bonaparte was born in Paris on 19 May 1858. He was educated for a military career and graduated from the École de Saint-Cyr, the French military academy. When the other Bonaparte princes were banished from France after Napoleon's defeat, Roland was allowed to remain, but was expelled from the French Army. He turned instead to the study of geography and the social sciences, including anthropology.

Bonaparte was trained in ethnology by Paul Broca, the French anthropologist and pioneer in brain surgery. His first practical fieldwork was to make anthropometric descriptions of the natives of Surinam, India, who were participating in the Colonial Exposition in Amsterdam in 1883. Photographs of the Surinam were taken by M. Hisgen of Amsterdam.[2]

In 1883 Bonaparte had photographs taken of visiting Omaha Indians for the Jardin d'Acclimation Exposition in Paris. These are reminiscent of the photographs taken of the Indian delegations to Washington DC, many years before. The faces of proud Omaha chiefs, attired in traditional ceremonial splendor, once more meet the heads of state as a nation.[3]

Bonaparte first traveled to the New World in 1887, to study and photograph the Indians of Mexico, Canada and the United States. He also sponsored expeditions to Africa, Asia and Australia, and had pictures taken of their native peoples at the 1889 Paris Universal Exposition.

By 1906, Bonaparte had amassed a collection of over seven thousand negatives, some of which were printed and distributed in portfolios. His North American Indians album, *Peaux Rouges*, had been printed in 1884. One of the copies was originally presented to the Anthropological Society of Washington, and later became part of the ethnographical photographic collections at the Smithsonian Institution.[4]

The Prince died on 15 April 1924 in Paris. Newspaper accounts of his death listed him as an ardent Republican, who had never aspired to the French throne. Instead he was cited for his honorary doctoral degrees from Uppsala and Cambridge Universities, and for his Presidencies of the French Geographical Society and International Aeronautical Federation. He was also known for his participation in the establishment of the League of Nations, after the First World War.

Bonaparte had been a great admirer of American institutions. During the First World War he had declared that, while proud to be a Frenchman, the next best thing he could have wished was to have been born a citizen of the United States. Most of all, he is remembered for his legacy of scholarly scientific publications, and for the haunting photographs he had made of the native peoples of the world.[5]

AMERICAN EXPOSITIONS

The New York World's Fair of 1853 was the first in America, and was formally opened on 14 July by President Franklin Pierce. Since the Indians were at the dawn of America's history, they played a distinctive role in the Fair. General Winfield Scott, a national hero and collector of Indian photographs, was one of the guests in attendance, but it seems that no photographs were exhibited on this occasion, only a gallery of paintings of different ethnic groups.[6]

THE CENTENNIAL EXPOSITION

The International Centennial Exposition was held in Philadelphia, Pennsylvania, from 10 May to 10 November 1876. It celebrated the hundredth anniversary of America's Independence by illustrating the progress in industry and technology that had since taken place. There had been more than a hundred years of war in America as well. In the West the Indian uprisings had reached their peak, and in one of history's sad ironies, that summer the Battle of the Little Bighorn took place. Colonel George Armstrong Custer and 264 soldiers of the US 7th Cavalry were killed by the Sioux in what would prove to be the last great Indian victory. Private and government expeditions were organized to collect materials for the Centennial, with the Smithsonian Institution participating for the first time. Objects were collected and photographs taken by the US Geographical and Geological Surveys to the American West. Before the field season of 1875, their official photographers, William Henry Jackson from the Hayden Survey and John K. Hillers of the Powell Survey, headed for the Grand Council held at Okmulgee, Indian Territory, where all nations living in the territory were represented. A sensitive ethnographic record was made by the two master photographers, documenting not only an historic event, but presenting a romantic view of warriors fresh from the warpath, at one of the last peace conferences of the nineteenth century.[7]

Jackson did not join the Hayden Survey of December 1875–February 1876, remaining in Washington instead, where he prepared material for a proposed historical and biographical catalog of photographs of seventy-five tribes of North American Indians for the Centennial. He also served as the US Geological Survey's representative at the Exposition. The Hayden Survey had its own exhibition stand of models of ruins from the Southwest, where the new dry-plate photographic process and new panoramic cameras were demonstrated. Jackson's photographs of the ancient cliff dwellings at Rio Mancos and Rio de Chelly and of the hot springs at Yellowstone National Park were also shown, and the stand won a bronze medal.[8]

THE WORLD COLUMBIAN INTERNATIONAL EXPOSITION

The World Columbian International Exposition was held from 1 May to 30 October 1893 in Chicago, to commemorate the fourth centenary of the discovery of America. As Professor Otis T. Mason, from the Smithsonian Institution's United States National Museum reported, 'Indeed, it would not be too much to say that the World's Columbian Exposition was one vast anthropological revelation. Not all mankind were there, but either in persons or pictures their representatives were.'[9]

The purpose of the Smithsonian's and the Bureau of American Ethnology's joint exhibition in the government building at this event was to 'teach the lesson of the beginnings of our modern industry. . . and the place which our aborigines occupied among the various peoples of the earth.'[10] Original drawings and maps (now in the British Museum) by the artist John White, of Indians on Roanoke Island off Carolina in 1585, were part of the exhibition. The illustrations were 'the first delineations by Englishmen of the natives of America showing their customs and costumes.' They conveyed the sense of place of the Indians, and their way of life at first contact.[11]

At the entrance to the joint exhibition a map was displayed, showing 'the condition of peoples of the North American continent at the time of discovery. . . in accordance with a linguistic map of the North American continent recently compiled by Major John Wesley Powell, Director of the Bureau of American Ethnology. . . showing the position of tribes and families at that time'.[12] In fact, the map resulted from Powell's official orders from the government to group the Indians linguistically in order to organize their removal to reservations more efficiently.

Inside the exhibition, ethnographical models (like those at the 1851 World Fair in London) were shown once again. However, now the figures of the Indians were not of 'savages' scalping white people, but of peaceful reservation Indians—Big Cow, a Kiowa; an Ute woman with her child in a cradleboard; and a man referred to as 'the Crow Artist'. There were also figures of Chief Red Cloud, Sitting Bull and Rosa White Thunder from the Sioux nation. Powell reported that they were 'one of the most striking features of the exhibition which met with high praise from American and foreign visitors and students and received the award of a medal and diploma for special merit.'[13] The models would later travel to the Columbia Historical Exposition in Madrid. The world would come to know the 'new' Indian — the reservation Indian.

Most professional photographers favored glass-plate cameras, and to take the photographs shown at this Exposition the large-format view cameras of William Henry Jackson and John K. Hillers had been used. But in 1888 the Kodak box camera had been invented, and there were now hundreds of amateur photographers vying to take pictures of the Indians. What had once been the domain of the masters soon became a circus, with everyone wanting what they believed would be the last photographs of the Indians.[14]

THE TRANS-MISSISSIPPI EXPOSITION

The Trans-Mississippi and International Exposition presented the products, industries and cultures of states west of the Mississippi. It was held at Omaha, Nebraska, from 1 June– 31 October 1898. President William J. McKinley opened the ceremonies, in grounds that became known as the 'Magic City'. Little more than a generation before, the Omaha Indians had lived peacefully on the land the Magic City now occupied.[15]

The 1898 Exposition was the most successful yet held in America. In the midst of an economic depression, and preceding the war with Spain over Cuba and the Philippines, it attracted over 2,500,000 visitors and deposited several hundred thousand dollars into the government's treasury. The latest in art and industry and all the advantages of white man's civilization were displayed, as evidence of what Manifest Destiny had accomplished in the West. By contrast, there was also a group of North American Indians representing tribes who had felt the impact of that Destiny—an impact so tremendous as to be almost inconceivable to those who had not experienced it.[16]

*Chief Wolf Robe, a Southern
Cheyenne, wearing a peace
medal. A portrait taken at the
Trans-Mississippi and
International Exposition, Omaha,
Nebraska, 1898.*
RINEHART AND MUHR

Most nineteenth-century expositions had exhibited a few Indians as curiosities of the past, but the 1898 Exposition had originally planned to show all the tribes that had been advanced under the national policy of assimilation. Alice Fletcher, a Smithsonian anthropologist, was appointed as the government's representative in charge of the Indian Education Exhibit, which included an Indian schoolhouse. As an added attraction, all the tribes were to be presented together at the first 'Indian Congress'.

The chiefs of all the Indian nations were invited to the Congress, including Turning Eagle, a Brule. At first he was reluctant to attend, and one of his friends, Jesse Hastings Bratley, a teacher and photographer, lamentedly reported that the Chief's participation meant his daughter had to be released from school to take over her father's chores. However, the Exposition was to have more far-reaching consequences than a few days of missed school.[17]

The idea for an Indian Congress had been conceived by Edward Rosewater, editor–publisher of the *Omaha Bee* newspaper, with the Department of the Interior holding overall responsibility for its execution. It placed Captain William A. Mercer, official agent for the nearby Omaha and Winnebago tribes, in charge, with James Mooney, from the Smithsonian Institution's Bureau of American Ethnology and the government's leading expert on Indian cultures at the time, appointed as a consultant. Frank A. Rinehart was hired on contract by the Bureau as the official photographer.

FRANK A. RINEHART

Rinehart was born in 1862 in Illinois, and died in 1929. His brother, Alfred Evan Rinehart, was also a photographer and the one-time partner of William Henry Jackson. From 1881 to 1885 Rinehart worked at his brother's studio and lived with Jackson's son, Fred, before opening his own studio in Omaha. The senior Jackson had honed his photographic skills to the highest order in the Civil War, on railroad surveys, and on scientific expeditions to the American West. His landscape photographs, together with his studio portraits of the Indians, had won him international acclaim. Watching Jackson work must have been a great inspiration to any novice photographer, and for Rinehart, who at twenty-nine was just beginning his career, Jackson must have had a tremendous impact, and could well have been one of the major reasons why Rinehart wanted to photograph the Indians.

Rinehart was given his own small studio in the grounds of the Exposition. His primary tool was an 8×10 glass-plate negative camera, equipped with a German lens, while skylights with hand-drawn shades gave the studio ideal lighting. It was an excellent atmosphere in which to take portraits of the Indians, away from the bustling activities of the fair.[18]

Rinehart had come to the Exposition with a specific purpose in mind. He had realized that it was a rare opportunity to study the Indians before they became absorbed into white culture. In his booklet, *Rinehart's Indians*, published in 1899, he stated:

'The camera. . . was ever busy recording scenes and securing types of these interesting people who with their savage finery are rapidly passing away. In a remarkably short time, education and civilization will stamp out the feathers, beads and paint—the sign language, the dancing—and the Indian of the past will live but in memory and pictures.'[19]

Rinehart began photographing the Indians when they first arrived in August, halfway through the Exposition. They continued to come in delegations and singly until its close. Mooney had planned for the Indian Congress (which he saw as a unique opportunity to educate the public about the Indians' traditional way of life, on a scale never previously attempted) to be held during the last week. Only a few years before, the massacre at Wounded Knee had signaled the end of the wars with the Indians, and Mooney and Rinehart believed, like so many of their contemporaries, that the remaining tribes would soon be gone. The Exposition seemed to be one of the last occasions when so many native peoples could participate and be photographed. As the project was of such a broad scope, Mooney had suggested to Rosewater that the tribes should be limited to those representing each different house-type of North American Indian. In total 545 Indian delegates from thirty-six tribes attended.[20]

The Indian Rights Association had endorsed the Indian Congress and approved its participation, provided it was 'carefully guarded from the designs of persons who might be disposed to divert it to personal schemes of money making or notoriety'.[21] However, during the course of the exhibition, Captain Mercer shifted the emphasis from education to entertainment, introducing the idea of sham battles starring the Indians. The initial show was to be held in connection with a convention of the Improved Order of Red Man (I.O.R.M.), a white fraternal secret order with costumes based on Indian dress. After the I.O.R.M. members arrived in Omaha, plans were finalized for an elaborate sham battle between the Indians and the Red Men on 10 August. Unfortunately, on the afternoon of the proposed mock warfare, the I.O.R.M. members advised Mercer that they would not participate. As the battle had been publicly advertised, Mercer made frantic efforts to save the event, even borrowing guns from local high school cadets. The Wild West Show participants at the Exposition, and some of the I.O.R.M. members who did show up, played the 'friendlies', while the 'hostiles' from the Indian Congress were led by Mercer.

The battle consisted of surprise attacks, counterattacks and retreats, with captives burned at the stake and daring rescues between the 'hostiles' and 'friendlies'. Following the battle, Indian women pretended to mutilate the dead bodies of their enemies. The Indians were paid half of the gate's receipts for their spending money, and the other half was collected by Mercer on behalf of the Exposition organizers.

The sham battles became wildly popular events. Gradually, other Indians joined the free-for-all, without the participation of outsiders. On 12 October, as an honorary guest at a sham battle, President McKinley met the participants in a grand parade, and enthusiastically endorsed the exhibition.[22]

James Mooney of the Smithsonian Institution had brought 106 delegates, their ponies, and a Wichita grass house from Oklahoma Territory to be constructed on the grounds of the Exposition. On 27 September 1898 Mooney reported back to the Smithsonian that the only ethnological features on site were the grass house and a tipi. The Indian Congress had

'rapidly degenerated into a Wild West Show with the sole purpose of increasing gate receipts. . . the only gain to ethnology will be in the chance to get a few pictures, to purchase some collections. The precedent may be of value in future expositions if the Bureau can secure control, but in this place an ethnologist's time is wasted and his labor lost.'[23]

Mercer, unlike Mooney, was aware that his audience was not yet ready to appreciate the diversity of the cultures it had so recently subjugated. Rinehart's photographs of the battles perpetuated the popular stereotype of hostile Plains Indians, yet most of the participants in the sham battles were members of the Sac and Fox and Flathead tribes, or from the pueblos of the Southwest. Only at the end of the Exposition were the Comanche, Kiowa, Wichita and Sioux delegates enticed to enter the mock warfare. In this atmosphere, Rinehart's photographs changed during the course of the Exposition from realistic portrayals of the Indians' way of life, as represented by the contemporary Indian leaders there in attendance, to images of romanticized warlike figures from the past.[24]

Despite the circus atmosphere, the Exposition was a nostalgic reunion for veterans from both sides of the Indian Wars. General Nelson Miles met his old friend and foe, the Apache chief Geronimo, who was still a prisoner of the War Department. The famous Sioux chiefs, Red Cloud and American Horse were there, together with White Swan, an Anglo, one of Custer's Crow scouts and the only known survivor of the Battle of the Little Bighorn. The Indians probably benefitted most from the opportunity to meet other Indians, and to exchange intertribal communications. The festivities included a Dog Feast, a Ghost dance and a Fire dance—not all the traditions had vanished.

During the last week of the Exposition, Rinehart was commissioned by the government to photograph the Congress delegates, but he was too busy photographing other events. The portraits of the delegates were actually taken by Adolph F. Muhr, a photographer who worked at Rinehart's Omaha studio.

ADOLPH F. MUHR

Muhr's photographs marked a unique historical event, and provide an unusual ethnographic record. He wrote in the Exposition catalogue that

> 'they [the Indians] were timid at first, hung back like children, but a little coaxing and a better acquaintance soon made smooth sailing. . . the acquaintance ripened into many warm friendships, and it is from conversations through the interpreters, that the information contained in this catalogue is compiled. The Ethnographical Introduction for each tribe is written from notes made at that time and verified from the limited sources at hand. I trust that any inaccuracies will be pardoned'.[25]

Muhr photographed the Salish delegation during the last two weeks of October 1898, but by the 27 October, the Exposition grounds were rapidly becoming deserted. A *World Herald* reporter lamented that 'what was once the warmest spot on the exposition grounds, the Indian Congress, is now rapidly becoming a deserted village, for by night none will be left save but two bands of Sioux'.[26]

Over two hundred photographs of seventy tribes were taken under Mooney's direction. As he reported,

> 'the work was done according to a systematic plan, the Indians being photographed in costume in tribal groups and singularly, in bust, profile, and full length, resulting in one of the finest collections of Indian portraits in existence. . . at the same time, the Indian name of each individual was obtained, with its interpretation, and some points of information concerning the tribe, with brief vocabularies of each language. . . .'[27]

The Bureau, which had paid half the photographers' fees, obtained a set of negatives. A further hundred prints were paid for by the Exposition management, with the copyright for them going to Rinehart.[28] Rinehart also copyrighted a second set of Muhr's photographs to be sold commercially by his studio, and there is some evidence that he later traveled to Indian reservations to supplement the Omaha photographs.

It is interesting to note which photographs Rinehart selected to publish in his portfolios. Most of the best portraits of the Indian chiefs are those taken by Muhr, while the ethnocentric captions seem to have been embellished by Rinehart from Mooney's and Muhr's notes. His own pictures are more documentary in nature, in contrast to Muhr's artistic compositions. The quality of Muhr's negatives, and the sensitivity they display towards his dignified sitters reflect his skill, his love of the work, his admiration for his subjects and their trust. It is not surprising that Muhr later worked with Edward S. Curtis, the supreme Pictorialist of North American Indians.

The Rinehart Indian Photographs, as they were popularly known, constitute one of the best photographic documentations of Indian leaders at the turn of the century. In them, the original purpose of the Indian Congress was realized, as they preserve the memory of the traditional North American Indians for the education of future generations.[29]

THE LOUISIANA EXPOSITION

The Louisiana Purchase Exposition was held in St Louis, Missouri, from 30 April to 1 December 1904, and celebrated the centennial anniversary of the purchase of the Louisiana territory by the United States from France. It was opened by Charles Warren Fairbanks, Vice President under Theodore Roosevelt.

Professor W. J. McGee, President of the American Anthropological Association, reported that 'the "living exhibits" at the Fair are in evolutionary order with the more advanced aborigines near the Indian School and terminating with the African pygmies and Igorots from the Philippines'. The 12–13 August were 'Anthropology Days' with ethnic dances, sports, and ceremonies performed in the Stadium.[30]

THE GERHARD SISTERS

Most unusually, two professional female photographers, Mamie and Emma Gerhard, successors to the Guerin and Canova studio in St Louis, worked at the Exposition, and succeeded in making a dynamic historic record of its participants.[31] Although not hired as official government photographers, they must have been endorsed by the Exposition management, as only photographers whose works were of professional quality, and who used large-format view cameras were granted a license to take pictures of the Indians and other participating ethnic groups. The throngs of amateur photographers were barred from formal picture taking.[32]

Like Adolph Muhr, the Gerhard sisters photographed the Indian leaders, including Geronimo and the Osage Chief Oh-lo-ho-walla, as well as the peoples of the Plains, the Southwest and California, in striking studio portraits. It is ironic that with the First World War only a decade away, the chiefs proudly wear the peace medals given to them, as leaders of separate nations, in past treaty negotiations with the government.

In addition to their portraits, the Gerhard sisters photographed the various activities taking place in the Exposition grounds. That they were highly skilled photographers is demonstrated by their interior shots of Cheyenne houses, and action shots of Hopi Snake and Eagle dancers. Together with Jesse Tarbox Beals, also from St Louis and one of the first women press photographers, the Gerhard sisters also took pictures of the native peoples of the Philippines, who were part of the anthropological exhibition.[33]

We know almost nothing about the Gerhard sisters other than their exceptional work. For now, they too are a silent voice in our history books. But, as they do for their subjects, their pictures speak for them. Their portraits of different ethnic groups are works of art. The human subject, the costumes, artifacts and animals become one. This is how a native American Indian artist would see and create an image. The Gerhards must have had a very special relationship with the peoples they photographed to be so aware of how they would view their world.

From the landscape views and ancient ruins photographed by Jackson we obtain a sense of time and space. The pictures of Bonaparte and Rinehart leave us with important historic ethnographical documentation. The art of Muhr and the Gerhards imparts to us the essence of the peoples. They all are haunting reminders of the traditional way of life of the North American Indians.

RIGHT
Hard Chief, an Omaha, at the Jardin d'Acclimation Exposition in 1883.
PRINCE ROLAND BONAPARTE

FAR RIGHT
Standing Bear (Montchou-Naji), an Omaha sub-chief, who represented the North American Indians at the Jardin d'Acclimation Exposition in Paris in 1883.
PRINCE ROLAND BONAPARTE

*Blackfoot/Piegan group,
photographed at the Trans-
Mississippi and International
Exposition, Omaha, Nebraska,
1898.*
RINEHART AND MUHR

*Two Apaches from the San
Carlos Agency, Arizona,
photographed at the Trans-
Mississippi and International
Exposition, Omaha, Nebraska,
1898. The man on the left was
called 'Long', the man on the
right 'Forgetting'.*
RINEHART AND MUHR

Nellie Jumping Eagle, a Sioux, photographed at the Louisiana Purchase Exposition, St Louis, Missouri, in 1904.
GERHARD SISTERS

Navaho couple at the Louisiana Purchase Exposition, 1904.
GERHARD SISTERS

Navajo Buck and Squaw
Copyrighted by
Gerhard Sisters
St Louis Mo.
1903.

Nancy Columbia, an Eskimo who
had been born at the 1893 World
Columbian Exposition,
photographed at the Louisiana
Purchase Exposition in 1904.
GERHARD SISTERS

An Eskimo group, including
Nancy Columbia (third from
right, standing), at the Louisiana
Purchase Exposition.
GERHARD SISTERS

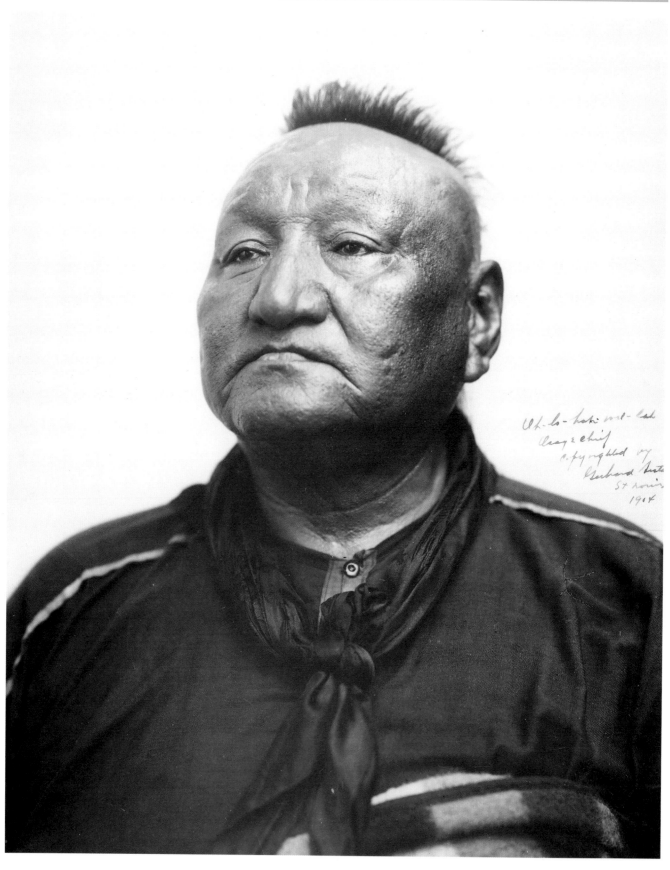

ABOVE

Chief Oh-lo-ho-walla of the Osage, photographed at the
Louisiana Purchase Exposition in 1904.
GERHARD SISTERS

RIGHT

Profile of an unidentified man, known as 'San Diego'. Louisiana
Purchase Exposition, 1904.
GERHARD SISTERS

95

Chief Cheyenne
Copy my Edit to
Gerhard Sio
Volume ...
1904

LEFT
*Richard Davis, the Cheyenne
informant for the anthropologist
George Dorsey. He is wearing a
costume later collected for the
Field Museum, Chicago, by the
photographers.*
GERHARD SISTERS

RIGHT
*Chief Trucha, an Apache,
photographed at the Louisiana
Purchase Exposition.*
GERHARD SISTERS

The Pictorialists

AFTER 1890, new processes and techniques were needed to ensure the survival of the professional photographer in the commercial world. Art salons and camera clubs devoted to a more artistic and interpretational style of photography were organized, and as a subject, their members rediscovered the American West. The Indians were of photographic interest not as a curiosity, as had been the case in the past, but because of those elements of artistic and ethnological significance they could lend to the new photographic medium.[1]

The members of these organizations were known as 'Pictorialists'. They experimented with new techniques—novel angles in composition, dramatic close-ups and lighting, soft focus lenses, abstract or non-existent backgrounds, added or omitted details, hand-tints or other coloring—in fact every possible means of manipulating the final result to make the image look more like an art form and less like a straightforward photograph.

The works of the Pictorialists all have high artistic values and share varying degrees of romanticism. To the best of their technical abilities and talents, they attempted to record and re-create what they believed to be the vanishing lifestyles of the North American Indians.

ROLAND REED

Roland W. Reed was born in 1864 in a log cabin on a farm in the Fox River Valley of Wisconsin, less than a hundred miles from what was to be the birthplace of Edward S. Curtis, perhaps the greatest Pictorialist photographer of North American Indians. The Menomini Indians used a trail near Reed's house to travel from their home on the north shore of Lake Poygan to the Indian camping grounds at Fond du Lac, Minnesota, where they gathered to hunt. As a child, Reed became acquainted with them, and longed to join the Indian boys who traveled along that forest path. It was a desire that never left him.

When Reed was seven years old, an incident occurred that, as he later recalled, instilled in him a high regard for the Indians. Reed wrote:

'In the spring of 1871, my schoolteacher and two of his pupils—boys about sixteen years old—took a canoe and went across the lake to gather some evergreens to decorate the schoolroom. Returning, their canoe overturned and the teacher was drowned. When nearly exhausted, [the boys] were discovered by three Indians who brought them ashore, made some broth for them, and then dug a hole deep in a haystack where they stayed for the night. This the Indians did to bring back their circulation and warm them up. I knew these Indians well, especially one called Thundercloud, who was chief of this band and who, after the rescue of the boys, became the hero of my boyhood days.'

'Bear's Belly', Arikara.
EDWARD S. CURTIS

Throughout his lifetime, Reed displayed a roving, adventurous nature. He traveled most of North America, leaving home at an early age and working on railroad gangs throughout Canada, the Midwest and the Southwest. Along the tracks he met and became friends with Indians from numerous tribes. Always, as he wrote, 'I don't know why, but no trip I could plan satisfied me unless it led into Indian country.'

Not all of his encounters with the Indians were friendly. On one of his trips, Reed was following the Mormon Trail toward Globe, Arizona. He spent the night with US Army troops, who were watching a village of Apaches. The next morning, Reed started alone for the San Carlos Agency, but took a wrong path, which led him into a camp of hostile Apaches. They treated him roughly, but let him leave. Reed later learned they had just killed a man. He commented 'I am sorry to say that I was not allowed through circumstances to photograph the Apache as I found him—as an Indian was really an Indian in those days.'

From 1890 onwards Reed taught sketching and drawing, producing landscapes and Indian portraits in crayon and pencil along the Great Northern Railroad tracks from North Dakota to Montana. The Blackfoot Indians of Montana were among his first subjects. He still had no knowledge of photography and had already noted that 'If I could master this seemingly easy way of making pictures (photography), I would have no trouble in getting all the Indian pictures I wanted.' His early sketches have not been found and were probably destroyed.

Reed got his wish, and from 1893 to 1897 became an apprentice to Daniel Dutro, a studio photographer of Havre, Montana. Reed and Dutro traveled together from town to town along the Great Northern Railroad tracks. Some of their Indian portraits were sold to the railroad's news department, to use in publicity material designed to attract passengers to the American West.[2]

In 1897 Reed left Dutro, and was hired by the Associated Press in Seattle to photograph the Yukon gold rush. He also attempted some photographs of the Alaskan Indians, but found the remaining native peoples totally uninspiring. 'They made such a poor impression on me that I left for the States on the first ship south in the spring without making any pictures worthwhile.'

Returning to the Midwest in 1900, Reed founded a studio in Bemidji, Minnesota, and later one in Ortonville. Now he pursued portrait photography with one purpose in mind— to accumulate enough funds to finance field trips among the Minnesota Chippewa (Ojibway), Plains Indians (Blackfoot, Cheyenne and Flathead) and the Southwest peoples (Navaho and Hopi).

Reed's first encounter with the Chippewa near his Bemidji studio did not go well. He had difficulty in obtaining pictures, and King Bird, the Chippewa leader, threw him out of the Red Lake village. Reed then went deeper into Indian territory, to the Cross Lake Indian School at Ponemah village, where he stayed in a shack, but still the Chippewa would have nothing to do with him. Finally, his camera itself enabled him to gain access to them. After patiently waiting for several days at Ponemah village, Reed was asked by two small girls from the Indian School to photograph their sick brother.

When Reed returned to the village several months later, he brought the finished print back with him. The father of the sick boy asked to see the photograph, then turned his back, walked away, and stood staring at it for some time. Finally, he asked Reed what the photograph would cost. Reed inquired about the boy, and only then learned that the child had died. As he presented the photograph to the father, Reed told him how glad he was that he had made the picture. Reed remembered 'That fine, old man gave me his hand, and from that time on, I was welcomed.'

By 1907, Reed had gained enough fame and fortune to close his studios and concentrate entirely on taking photographs of the Indians. He was, he wrote, 'determined to devote all my strength and energy to document the Indian heritage.' It was Reed's intention to produce a volume of portraits which would be a definitive photographic record of the North American Indians.[3]

Among his first subjects were the Piegan of Montana, whom Reed photographed in 1908. The Piegan had lost their traditional ceremonial and social life, and Reed constructed his version of these people's history with the help of elders who remembered the 'old' ways. Reed's portraits and landscapes, containing few people in very formal poses, reflect the pride and dignity that he wished to restore to them.

In 1915 Reed and the writer James Willard Schultz collaborated on an illustrated book entitled *Blackfeet Tales of Glacier National Park*. They took a group of Indians, with costumes and studio paraphernalia, into the romantic setting of the park (where the Blackfoot had never in fact lived) and re-created the stories told to them by the Blackfoot elders. Reed photographed these Indians as if they had lived as part of this natural environment. The throngs of tourists who visited the park that year are nowhere to be seen, and the book was to influence a generation of readers who loved romantic tales of the old American West.

'Into the Wilderness'
A Blackfoot group in Glacier National Park, Montana, 1915. Such images were used to illustrate Blackfeet Tales of Glacier National Park.
ROLAND REED

Daisy Norris, a Blackfoot, with baby carrier.
ROLAND REED

During the same year Reed also provided fifteen 36″×48″, one 36″×30″, and six 36″×24″ bromide prints for the Great Northern Railroad's building at the Panama–Pacific Exposition in San Francisco, California. One of these, 'The Pottery Maker' (Hopi), won a gold medal. Later that year, Reed's photographs of Pueblo and Navaho Indians were exhibited at the International Exposition held in San Diego, where he may also have had a studio, as he wrote later in his life that his negatives were in storage there.[4]

In 1932, twenty-five years after he dedicated his life's work to recording the North American Indians, Reed concluded that 'It is no longer possible to obtain authentic Indian pictures. The Indians' historic costumes and accoutrements have all been sold to tourists and few examples of pure racial types are still alive.'[5]

Reed was not a prolific photographer. He believed his work was an art form, and that it took patient years of refinement to produce the few images he wished to create. One photograph could take him weeks or months to produce. Consequently, his output was never voluminous—during his first three years among the Indians, he made only a score of negatives. In his later years, Reed considered that a dozen superior photographs represented a good day's work.

In a letter, Reed explained how he obtained his photographs:

'In approaching the Indian for the purpose of taking his picture, it is necessary to respect his stoicism and reticence which have so often been the despair of the amateur photographer. A friend once characterized my method of attack as indicative of Chinese patience, book-agent persistence, and Arab subtlety. In going into a new tribe with photographic paraphernalia, although I hire ponies and guides, I never once suggest the object of my visit.

When the Indians, out of curiosity, at last inquire about my work, I reply casually "Oh, when I'm home, I'm a picture-taking man." Perhaps in a few days an Indian will ask. . . "Could you make our pictures?" My reply is non-commital . . . "I don't know . . . Perhaps." "Would you try?" "Sometime, when I feel like making pictures." Further time elapses, apparently the picture-taking man has forgotten all about making pictures until an Indian friend reminds him of his promise. Then the time for picture-taking has arrived.'[6]

Reed turned down an offer of $15,000 for 200 of his negatives, rather than have them used for advertising. The only publication rights believed to have been granted by Reed were to the *National Geographic Magazine*. In 1933 he planned to reproduce his photographs to sell to schools, libraries and Boy Scout groups, as he only wanted his pictures used for educational purposes.

Reed never achieved his dream of publishing his North American Indian photographs. Unlike Edward S. Curtis and Joseph Kossuth Dixon, he did not have access to the influential circles of high society, nor was he acquainted with scholars who studied the Indians. There were no wealthy patrons such as John Pierpont Morgan, Edward Harriman or Rodman Wanamaker to sponsor Reed's expeditions into Indian territory. He had to use his own savings and the revenue from photographic sales. But he still produced a monumental study, and is remembered as one of the most important of the Pictorialists.

Upon Reed's death in 1934, a collection of about seventy negatives of the Chippewa (Ojibway), Cheyenne and Blackfoot Indians was inherited by a cousin, Roy E. Williams. Williams used them in lectures to school children. In 1977 the heirs of Williams's estate sold the collection and rights to the Kramer Gallery in St Paul, Minnesota, where the negatives now reside. The Kramer Gallery has acquired additional Reed photographs to bring its collection to 180 glass-plate negatives, and plans to publish them in a five-part catalog of Reed's Indian work.[7] His work lives on through their efforts.

JOSEPH KOSSUTH DIXON AND THE WANAMAKER EXPEDITIONS OF CITIZENSHIP

During the years before the First World War, when patriotic feelings ran high, a group of concerned American citizens attempted to alleviate the despair of life on the Indian reservations. Expeditions to the West were organized once again—this time not by the government, but by private enterprise. Their mission was not one of discovery and scientific study of the land and its resources as in the past, but rather aimed to save the Indians from cultural extinction. Photographs and film footage taken on these expeditions were used to publicize Indian history, in order to give impetus to a national campaign to make them citizens. At the time many people believed that citizenship was the North American Indians' only chance of survival.

The financial support behind this movement was given by Rodman Wanamaker, heir to the Philadelphia department store dynasty, who commissioned Joseph Kossuth Dixon, a Doctor of Law, to serve as expedition leader. Dixon was a highly skilled photographer in the best tradition of the Pictorialists. His son, Rollin Lester Dixon, led the motion picture unit.

The first expedition was to the Valley of the Little Bighorn, Montana, in 1908, where the Dixons wanted to shoot a movie version of Longfellow's *Hiawatha*. The movie was made on the Crow Reservation, with Indians acting out the characters. While Rollin filmed, Joseph Dixon took over a thousand still photographs of the landscape and daily life of the Indians. The Wanamaker store was to publish a North American Indian Primer using 80 photographs from this expedition, with copies being distributed to schools where they were used as textbooks.

A second Wanamaker Expedition returned to the valley in 1909. The Census that year had reported a 65% decline in the Indian population. Wanamaker and Dixon, like so many of their contemporaries, believed the traditional North American Indians were destined to disappear entirely. Tribal elders also felt that they were the last generation to remember the traditional ways. They knew that they would soon die, and their people would be assimilated into the white man's culture. They were even fearful for the survival of their children. Chief White Horse of the Sioux told Dixon '. . . I was one of the first to send my children to Hampton, Virginia, to school. They all came home and died of consumption.'[8] White Horse had seven children.

The 1909 expedition was endorsed by President William Howard Taft. The Commissioner of Indian Affairs, Robert Grosvenor Valentine, also expressed his full cooperation. Dixon once again served as leader. The aim was to record the final meeting of the surviving chiefs from almost all of the Western reservations—Apache, Blackfoot, Cayuse, Cheyenne, Comanche, Creek, Crow, Gros Ventre, Kiowa, Umatilla and Sioux—in the last great Indian Council.

The chiefs, who were between fifty and eighty years old, represented the last generation to remember a way of life that had altered drastically. The Council was an opportunity for them to tell their history for future generations. Dixon recorded their stories and took their photographs, later publishing some of them in his book, *The Vanishing Race.*

On this expedition, the Dixons re-created the Battle of the Little Bighorn in still photographs and film. Custer's surviving Crow scouts—Curly, Goes Ahead, Hairy Moccasin and White-Man-Runs-Him, the opposing Cheyenne chief Two Moons and the Sioux chief Runs-the-Enemy played themselves in this version of the historic battle.

To quell the fears of those who believed that the gathering would evoke the Indians' days of glory in such a way as to incite further disastrous warfare, Dixon responded that the expedition's purpose was to record authentic Indian customs and show the 'highest ideals of peace', in that old warriors who had once loved battle now embraced peace instead.

Dixon promised the chiefs that the pictures he took would be preserved in the nation's capital for future generations. For those who attended this last great Council, it was a nostalgic meeting of many nations. As Chief Red Cloud reported:

'I think this is a great and good thing. Good things have come to us from the white man. . . The coming of this man to make these pictures, to be preserved in Washington and to be shown in great cities, means good to us, because the generations to come

Joseph Kossuth Dixon playing President Woodrow Wilson's speech to the leaders of the Umatilla in northern Oregon, 1913.

will know of our manners and customs. It is good besides, to meet all these chiefs who are as brothers to one another. We have never met them before; we shall never see their faces again, and it is therefore, I think, a great and good thing to have this last council of the chiefs.'[9]

On 12 May 1909, Wanamaker proposed to Congress that a national monument should be erected in the harbor of New York to honor the memory of the North American Indians. Dixon testified at the hearings, and an Act of Congress for the monument was signed by President Taft on 8 December 1911. It was to take the form of a colossal bronze statue, larger than the Statue of Liberty, of an Indian with right hand uplifted in the peace sign. Plans for the monument moved ahead for the next two years.

On the anniversary of George Washington's birth, on 22 February 1913, ground-breaking ceremonies took place on a hilltop at Fort Wadsworth, Staten Island, New York (now the terminus of the Verrazano–Narrows Bridge). The President, Cabinet members, diplomats, Army and Navy officers, and representatives of citizens from all walks of life watched as thirty-two chiefs from eleven different tribes signed a Declaration of Allegiance to the United States government and, for the first time in their history, hoisted an American flag. Dixon reported that 'These grizzled old warriors as heroes of the chase declared that never before had they felt that they were part of this country.' At the ceremony, Red Hawk of the Oglala Sioux spoke for the chiefs:

'It is my strong belief. . . that we were created by the Great Spirit to live in this country. You white men found me here. I am here, today. I was the ruler here in that time when you first crossed the great Atlantic, and I thought you had merely come as a visitor. From that time to this day you have improved our country. You have made me a part of this country. . . we have been taught in our Indian ways to love one another as brothers. I hope you have been taught, too. Let us join hands and minds to help us get out of the rut for the rest of our lives.'[10]

During a trip to the East Coast in 1913, to attend the inauguration ceremonies for President Woodrow Wilson, an Indian delegation traveled from Washington DC to Philadelphia, to attend an honorary luncheon in the office of Rodman Wanamaker at his store. Mountain Chief, a Blackfoot, presented Wanamaker with a buffalo-tooth necklace, and he was also given an Indian name, 'High Crow', a honor never before bestowed on a white man by this tribe.

That same year, inspired by these ceremonies, Wanamaker sponsored the Expedition of Citizenship, which was again led by Joseph Dixon. His mission was to take the American flag, as a symbol of citizenship, from Fort Wadsworth, the site of the proposed national monument, to every one of the existing 189 tribes. Dixon was to give a flag to each tribe to raise over their homes, as a re-enactment of the ceremony in New York. For six months, Dixon traveled the country by train. At each stop he played a speech by President Wilson on the new portable recording machine, just invented by Thomas Edison's company. In that speech, Wilson included the reassurance that 'The Great White Father now calls you his "Brother", not his "Children".'

Twenty thousand miles were covered on the expedition, primarily in a private railroad car which also served as a darkroom. Joseph Dixon led a four-man photographic unit, consisting of himself, his son Rollin, John D. Scott, a New York photographer, and W. B. Cline, another photographer who was loaned from George Eastman's studio in Rochester,

New York. There is still a controversy over who actually took the pictures, but their authorship does not matter. It is only important that they were taken.

The purpose of the expedition he financed was set out by Wanamaker in his foreword to *The Vanishing Race*:

'In undertaking these expeditions to the North American Indian, the sole desire has been to perpetuate the life story of the first Americans and to strengthen in their hearts the feeling of allegiance and friendship for their country ... for this purpose ... expeditions were sent forth to gather historic data and make picture records of their manners, customs, their sports and games, their warfare, religion, and the country in which they live.'[11]

Dixon's own great love for the Indians and the romantic viewpoint that permeated all his photographs was conveyed in the dedication of this book:

'To the man of mystery —
the earth his mother —
the sun his father —
a child of the mountains and the plains
a faithful worshipper in the great world cathedral —
now a tragic soul haunting the shores of the western ocean
my brother, the Indian.'[12]

Pictures from the 1913 expedition were exhibited at the San Francisco Panama–Pacific Exposition of 1915. Former President Theodore Roosevelt opened the show in July, stating that the photographs were 'the finest expression of the Indians in photographic art' that he had seen. Dixon lectured at the exhibit, three times a day for over five months, to more than 3,000,000 people. Prints were also offered for sale to the general public, marking what was probably the first time exposition photographers were able to make a profit in this way at such an event.

Further expeditions, and the construction of the national monument were halted due to the outbreak of the First World War. In patriotic fervor, the citizenship movement led by Wanamaker and Dixon resulted in a Congressional act to authorize the organization of ten or more regiments of North American Indians for the US Army. Indian warriors who had fought on horseback against the military were now to become a part of its cavalry.

After the First World War, the nation's depressed economy further stalled plans for the monument, but Wanamaker and Dixon continued to pressurize the government over the issue of granting citizenship to the Indians. Wanamaker, now a US Army Colonel, and representatives of the War and Interior Departments attended Indian ceremonies to honor war heroes of the past, and Indian delegates paid a moving tribute at the grave of the Unknown Soldier in Arlington National Cemetery. Moreover, on 10 November 1921, at the Willard Hotel in Washington DC, the Crow tribe adopted General Diaz, commander-in-chief of the Italian armies, as one of its members, and honored him as a fellow soldier. As warrior to warrior, Chief Plenty Coups presented Diaz with the honors of Indian regalia and bestowed upon him an Indian name, 'A-Cheea Ohause', or his own name, 'Plenty Coups'. The photographs taken at this event brought public attention to the Indians' own history of courage, and their place in America's military history.

On all three Wanamaker expeditions, the Dixons' used Kodak 3A and Graflex cameras.

Over eleven thousand negatives on glass-plate and nitrate film, and 50 miles of motion picture film were produced. The film has since deteriorated, but the prints remain. In 1965, researchers for the American Society of Magazine Photographers also discovered a number of the Dixons' photographs which had been presented to the American Museum of Natural History in 1938 by the Wanamaker family.[13]

The Wanamaker expeditions took place at a time when national guilt at what Manifest Destiny had done to the Indians was at its peak. The results were intended to be used as a message of healing for both sides of the cultural clash. The national monument was never built, but the collection of photographs taken on the Wanamaker expeditions stand as the Indians' true monument. Overshadowed as they are by the work of Edward S. Curtis, the Dixons' evocative images are frequently disregarded, but it was largely due to their ethnographic power that full citizenship was finally granted to the North American Indians in 1924.

EDWARD S. CURTIS

Edward S. (Sheriff) Curtis was born on 16 February 1868, in Wisconsin. Just nine months after his birth, Chief Red Cloud signed the Fort Laramie Peace Treaty to end the Sioux Indian wars. That same year, the United States government declared that an '"Indian problem" no longer existed . . . and no Indian nation or tribe . . . within the United States shall be acknowledged or recognized as an independent nation or power.' Indians as 'wards of the State' were being forced onto reservations and now were fighting for their very existence.

Curtis's family moved to Minnesota shortly after his birth, where he grew up in a region rich in Indian lore. The Chippewa (Ojibway), Menomini and Winnebago were his neighbors. Although most of the frontier wars were over, massacres of both Indians and whites were still reported in the daily newspaper. The transcontinental railroad was near completion, and the bison were gone from the Plains. Curtis grew up witnessing the effects of America's Manifest Destiny.

Curtis built his own crude camera while still in his teens, and taught himself photographic techniques from *Wilson's Photographics: A Series of Lessons Accompanied by Notes on all Processes which are Needful in Photography*, a self-help guide. During his early years in Minnesota, Curtis may have worked for a time as an apprentice in a St Paul photographic studio, and may also have attempted, unsuccessfully, to run his own photography business.

In the autumn of 1887, Curtis and his father, the Reverend Johnson Curtis, set out for Washington Territory in the hope of improving the family's circumstances. A year later they sent for the rest of the family: mother Ellen, sister Eva, and brothers Ray and Ashael. When the Reverend Curtis died of pneumonia shortly afterwards, Edward, at the age of twenty, was left with full responsibility for the family. He farmed, fished, dug clams, and did chores for neighbors to earn enough to provide food and shelter, yet despite his straitened circumstances in these early years, he nonetheless somehow managed to buy his first camera from a man who needed a grubstake for a trip to the California gold fields.

In 1891, the year the US Census Bureau announced the Western Frontier was officially closed, Curtis purchased a $150 share in the photographic studio of Cedarholm, Sanstrom and Rothi in Seattle, by borrowing against the family homestead. He formed a new partnership with Rasmus Rothi, and the studio became known as Rothi and Curtis, Photographers. This partnership had lasted barely a year when Curtis entered a new arrangement with Thomas Guptill, trading as Curtis and Guptill, Photographers and Photogravers. Both young men did portrait work, while Curtis also engraved the printing plates used to reproduce photographs and Guptill's drawings for local publications.

Curtis's business grew rapidly, as did his family. In the spring of 1892 he married Clara Phillips, who brought three members of her family to live with them. One of her sisters, Sue Phillips Gates, worked as a photo-printer for Curtis and Guptill, as did a first cousin, William W. Phillips. A third Phillips, Nellie, also worked for the studio. The household still included Curtis's mother and his younger brother and sister. In addition, Curtis and Clara would soon have four children of their own to support. The financial burden this imposed upon Curtis was to haunt him throughout his career.

In 1897 Guptill went his own way, and the business became Edward S. Curtis, Photographer and Photograver. At that point Curtis's younger brother Ashael was working in the engraving shop, and his pictures and journalistic reports of the Alaskan gold rush fever in Seattle's docks show that he, too, was a talented and skilful photographer.

There is still a controversy over the commencement of Curtis's Indian photographs, the first of which possibly date from around 1895. It is certain that 'Princess' Angeline, as she was known, was one of his first subjects. The elderly daughter of the Squamish chief from whom Seattle had taken its name, Angeline lived in a waterfront cabin and eked out a living by having her picture taken. She had a reputation as a character and was reported to have thrown clams at the local sheriff's house numerous times. When Curtis gave her a dollar to allow him to photograph her, her reported comment to him was 'More easy work than dig clams.'[14]

Besides the expanding family business, Curtis's reputation as a master photogapher was also growing rapidly. In 1896, he and his partner's exhibition of portraits at the National Photographers' Convention in Chautaugqua, New York, had won a bronze medal for their excellence in posing, lighting and tone. Later that year, local newspapers referred to them as the leading photographers on Puget Sound, and their work was to be found in nearly every home in the Pacific Northwest. It was also reported that a new type of photographic process, where the print was developed on a gold or silver plaque, had originated with Curtis and Guptill. The results were described as 'brilliant and beautiful beyond description'. These plaques may have been the forerunners of the goldtone pictures for which Curtis would later become famous.[15]

Curtis and his friend and fellow photographer, Duncan Inverarity, began photographing the Puget Sound Indians who made their way to work in the hop fields south of Seattle. Curtis also spent time on the Tulalip Reservation in Washington Territory taking pictures, including one of an Indian policeman and his wife. He gained access to the Indians and won their confidence by treating them as equals. Curtis explained 'I said, "we" not "you" . . . in other words, I worked with them and not at them.'[16]

In 1898, Curtis won first place in the Genre Class at the National Photographic Convention and the next year again won first place honors for 'Evening on Puget Sound', 'The Clamdigger', and 'The Mussel Gatherer'. Curtis's work traveled with other Grand Prize winners on a two-year tour of foreign countries, winning him an international reputation.[17]

The Curtis family business also kept up with contemporary issues. A local newspaper reported that the brothers were to take 3,000 pictures in the Yukon region, a business venture on a gigantic scale, reflecting the tremendous interest at that time in the Alaskan gold fields: 'This collection of photographs, when completed, will be the largest and best attempted of this wonderful country.'[18]

THE YUKON EXPEDITION (1897–99)

The Yukon Expedition not only presented a great physical risk but a financial one as well. The rent for Curtis's family home was $29 a month, whereas the photographic equipment alone for this trip would cost several hundred dollars. All the family members pitched in to

'Princess' Angeline, the elderly daughter of Chief Siahl (Seattle). She was for many years a familiar figure on the streets of the city, and provided one of the photographer's first Native American subjects.
EDWARD S. CURTIS

raise the money for the gear, which included an oversize tent and specially made photographic plates.

Before the end of 1897, Ashael had left on the passenger ship *Rosalie* to sail to Skagway, Alaska. He would stay in the north taking pictures for the next two years, sending the negatives back to Seattle for printing. Unfortunately, upon his return, he promptly claimed ownership of his glass plates. As was often done, both then and now, a photographic firm usually held copyright over images produced by its employees, but Ashael wanted control of his own work. The Curtis brothers quarreled over possession of the photographs, and ended by not speaking to each other for the rest of their lives.

In March 1898, the *Century Illustrated Monthly Magazine* printed an article by Curtis on the Yukon, which was probably his first published writing. Although credit was given to him for seven of the accompanying photographs, there is no indication that he had been to the Yukon himself at this time (this is probably the reason why Ashael wished to retain the rights to the photographs taken there). Later that year, however, a chance meeting on the slopes of Mount Rainier would unexpectedly widen both Curtis's horizons and his ambitions.

On one of his treks to the mountains, Curtis stumbled upon the members of a government commissioned party, who were lost. After leading them to his camp, Curtis discovered the leaders to be the nationally known naturalist and physician, Dr C. Hart Merriman, chief of the US Biological Survey, Dr George Bird Grinnell, naturalist and writer-editor on the Plains Indians for *Forest and Stream* magazine, and Gifford Pinchot, a pioneer conservationist and chief of the Division of Forestry. After guiding them safely through the mountains, Curtis took them to his Seattle studio to show them the hundreds of photographs of the landscape and Indians he had taken. They were impressed, and in the spring of 1899 Merriman and Grinnell invited Curtis to serve as official government photographer on a scientific expedition to Alaska.[19]

THE HARRIMAN EXPEDITION (1899)

The Harriman Expedition to Alaska had originally been planned as a luxury vacation for Edward Harriman, a railroad tycoon. The previous year, Harriman had outmaneuvered fellow entrepreneur, J. Pierpont Morgan, to gain control of the Union Pacific Railroad. The much-needed rest ordered by his doctor became an opportunity for the uneducated Harriman to make a contribution to the scientific world and establish his name academically in social and business circles. It was also a chance to survey routes for a new trans-Alaskan railroad.

Harriman had sought the assistance of Merriman in Washington DC to set up the expedition. Twenty-three of America's leading authorities in various fields were recruited, mostly from the prestigious Cosmos Club. They included the naturalist John Muir and the landscape artist Robert Swain Gifford. There was also the ship's staff of eighty-nine, the Harriman family, and an entourage of medical personnel, stenographers, hunters and packers—all of whom would spend two months cruising the Alaskan coast.

In Seattle the party was joined by Curtis and his photographic assistant, Duncan Inverarity, and then departed for the Alaskan wilderness. During the voyage, Curtis developed a special interest in the different ethnic groups he encountered, but Merriman took almost all the ethnographic photographs at the dozen stops they made along the way.

Curtis took only a few Indian images on the Harriman Expedition. However, he and Inverarity printed all of Merriman's negatives, and probably discussed their contents with him. In addition, Curtis observed Harriman recording Indian languages and songs on his new wax cylinder machine. He also listened to Grinnell's shipboard lectures on his twenty years of experience with the Blackfoot Indians.

The Harriman Expedition was the last great nineteenth-century survey to ascertain the economic potential of America's frontier. It was undertaken just as the experience of Manifest Destiny was being re-assessed. In the late 1890s, the West became a romantic symbol for traditional American culture, as it had been before the age of industry and technology altered it. The rugged frontier had been transformed from a wild, desolate land, temporarily inhabited by trappers, hunters, cowboys and Indians, into the permanent home of strong, self-reliant individuals—the settlers.[20]

The harsh, realistic details of exploration and pioneering were never depicted in the expedition's photographs of Alaska. Almost all of the 5,000 photographs were of geological formations, mostly taken by Curtis himself. But Curtis's relationship with Harriman, the most powerful railroad tycoon of the time, Grinnell, a leading ethnographic expert on the Indians, and other members of the survey party greatly altered his life. He began to learn the techniques of scientific investigation and ethnographic study of other cultures, and to make his first contacts among wealthy and influential patrons back East. These would later prove invaluable to him.

It took fifteen years and thirteen volumes to publish all the findings of the Harriman Expedition. Two volumes were made available to the general public and eleven were for professional scholars. In addition, Harriman commissioned Curtis to produce a special souvenir album of his photographs for the expedition members.[21]

In early 1900, Curtis sold his engraving business and took over the studio of Frank La Roche, another well-known photographer of Alaska and the Indians. That summer, he accepted an invitation from Grinnell and traveled with him to Browning, Montana. They went on horseback to an encampment of Blood, Blackfoot and Algonquin tribes, drawn up in a circle for their annual Sun dance. Everywhere was the bustle of wagons, horses and families, as the Indians gathered together. Curtis remarked

'Neither house nor fence marred the landscape, and the broad, undulating prairie stretching away toward the Little Rockies . . . was carpeted with tipis . . . It was at the start of my concentrated effort to learn about the Plains and to photograph their lives, and I was intensely affected.'

This Sun dance was the last held for many years. The ceremony was outlawed by the government because of its 'barbarous cruelty'. Curtis described it as 'wild, terrifying, and elaborately mystifying'.[22]

From 1901 to 1906, Curtis took pictures of the Northwest, Southwest and Plains Indians. He gave his first formal exhibition of Indian photographs at his studio gallery in 1903, advertising them as 'the latest images of the Mohave, Zuni, Supia and Apache'. From the beginning of the twentieth century until the First World War, the public's interest in photographs and information about the Indians was at its peak, and the stage was set for Curtis to emerge as America's leading photographer of the subject.

What made Curtis unique among photographers of North American Indians at this time was his highly skilled art style combined with his concern for ethnographic details. Curtis did not take pictures of semi-acculturated people wearing blue jeans and cowboy hats in the streets of Seattle, but traveled to remote reservations to photograph the Indians in traditional dress, still practicing ancient ceremonies in their own environment.

For his first pictures, Curtis asked the Indians to re-enact famous battles or conduct ceremonies for his camera. He then de-emphasized any assimilation that had taken place with the culture of the white man, sometimes by the removal of contemporary dress and objects, in order to create romantic images of the historical American West. His Indian subjects, many of whom were demoralized by reservation life, willingly participated in the picture making as if they too wanted to recapture their past daily and spiritual life of freedom, now overcome by outsiders.

Curtis lived among the Indian people and studied their ways in depth, and by doing so gained their trust and friendship. The Hopi called him 'the man who sleeps on his breath', after they had observed him blowing up his inflatable mattress. To the Sioux, he was 'Bashole Washte' (Pretty Butte – a butte being an isolated hill or small mountain), perhaps for his handsome looks, or perhaps for the beautiful pictures he took of their environment.[23]

In 1904, Adolph F. Muhr, who had photographed the delegates at the Trans-Mississippi Exposition of 1898, was hired by Curtis as his darkroom assistant. Muhr appears not to have taken photographs of the Indians at this time, handling the laboratory work instead. Curtis called him 'the genius in the darkroom', and turned all the printing of negatives over to him. Later, Muhr would be assisted by two female photographers, Imogene Cunningham and Ella McBride. When he died in 1913, McBride took over the management of the Curtis studio, together with Curtis's seventeen-year-old daughter, Beth.[24]

Curtis wanted, most of all, to gain the approval of Smithsonian Institution officials in presenting his photographs as being both scientific and artistic, and therefore in 1904 he traveled to the East Coast to discuss his Indian work with leading American ethnologists. He felt he could provide new ethnographic detail for professional anthropologists, as well as a beautiful record designed to inform the general public. It is evident that by this point at least, Curtis had decided upon a large-scale, multi-volume study of the Indians in which he would present his photographs. His aim in doing this was that the Indians should not 'by future generations be forgotten, misconstrued, too much idealized, or too greatly underestimated.' Curtis made it clear that he regarded this work as essential:

'The passing of every old man or woman means the passing of some tradition, some knowledge of sacred rites possessed by no other; consequently, the information that is to be gathered, for the benefit of future generations . . . must be collected at once or the opportunity will be lost for all time. It is this need that has inspired the present task.'[25]

Throughout his career, Curtis would fight to be accepted by scholars of North American Indians. One of his first supporters was Frederick Webb Hodge, a noted anthropologist at the Smithsonian Institution's Bureau of American Ethnology (BAE), whom Curtis visited early in 1904. Hodge was writing and editing one of the BAE's major publications, *The Handbook of the American Indians North of Mexico*. He was also editor of the *American Anthropologist*, and had done extensive fieldwork in the Southwest with the Hemenway Expedition, as well as two seasons with A. C. Vroman, the noted photographer, in the 1890s. Hodge agreed to be the General Editor of Curtis's proposed volumes at the rate of $7 per thousand words. The sum was often difficult to pay, but for Curtis this was a prestigious, fortunate alliance.

On the same trip to the East, Curtis went to see Walter Page at Doubleday Publishers in New York, in order to discuss the publication of his Indian photographs. His first attempt failed; Page refused on the grounds that 'the market's full of 'em. Couldn't give them away', but Curtis persisted, and when Page finally saw the photographs, he changed his mind and agreed to print them in lots of 5,000. Curtis then traveled to the Southwest for fieldwork among the Navaho of Arizona. The success of his trips was reported in the *Seattle Times*:

'. . . Government scientists who have devoted a lifetime to the study of Indians chanced to mention the great Yabachai dance. It seems this dance is hidden among the most sacred rites of the Navaho . . . Smithsonian Institution men told Mr. Curtis that pictures of the dance would be priceless from the standpoint of the Indian historian.'[26]

On 15 March 1905, Curtis received a letter from Matilda Coxe Stevenson, well known for her ethnographical work among the Zuni, who was on the staff of the BAE. She wrote in understanding of the difficulties he faced in his work and with appreciation of his efforts:

'Only the few will record for future generations the true history of the vanishing race, for without certain qualities it is simply impossible to succeed in obtaining the confidence of the Indians. It is a continual wonder to me that you have in so few years passed within the doors of the inner life of so many tribes.'

Other nineteenth-century ethnographers, such as Franz Boas, Columbia University's first professor of anthropology and famous for his work with the Northwest peoples, and James Mooney, the BAE's leading expert on most Indian cultures, including the Plains tribes, would challenge the competence of Curtis's fieldwork. To them, he would always remain an outsider.

In the summer of 1905, Curtis went to the Coleville Reservation in Washington Territory for the dedication of a monument to the late Nez Perce chief, Hin-mah-too-yah-lat-keht, or Thunder Rolling in the Mountains, popularly known as Chief Joseph. The chief and his nephew, Red Thunder, had been photographed in Curtis's studio only two years before, when Chief Joseph had been in Seattle to deliver a speech supporting his crusade for the Nez Perce to be allowed to return to their homelands. Chief Joseph's body was to be reburied in a sacred ceremony in the Okanogan Hills at the same time as the monument dedication. There were two other photographers present for the ceremonies: Edward Latham, physician and agent for the reservation, and Lee Moorhouse, a former Indian agent whose pictures had been shown at the St Louis Exposition in 1904. The Nez Perce elders strongly objected to the presence of photographers, and it took many hours of 'parleying' to gain their acceptance of the cameras. It was reported that at one point, Curtis had to threaten to use a six-shooter before permission was granted for the photographs to be taken.

After the ceremonies, Curtis went to South Dakota to visit the Sioux. Starting at the scene of the tragedy of Wounded Knee, which had taken place only fifteen years before, Chief Red Hawk and twenty of the men who had lived through and vividly remembered the Indian wars went north to the Sacred Hills, to take Curtis back to that world. During the three-week trip, he took his famous photograph, 'Oasis in the Badlands', of Red Hawk watering his horse on the prairie. Upon Curtis's departure, he promised the men who had ridden with him to give a feast in remembrance when he returned. Two years later he kept that promise, only this time he would meet hundreds of Sioux, staging ancient rites and old battles for his camera.

On 25 June 1907, thirty-one years after the Battle of the Little Bighorn, Curtis and his son, Harold, went overland from Wounded Knee to the Crow Reservation in Montana. There they rode with surviving Crow scouts of the US 7th Cavalry — White-Man-Runs-Him, Hairy Moccasin and Goes Ahead, and the Cheyenne and Sioux who had been their enemies. Up to this time, Curtis had been mainly living with and learning about the Indian peoples who had been fishermen, hunters and farmers. Now, he was introduced to the militant warriors of the Plains tribes. He started to notice the discrepancies between the war stories

'Coming for the Bride', Quagyuhl (Kwakiutl). A still from the silent film In the Land of the Headhunters, *produced by the photographer and his staff between 1910 and 1914.*
EDWARD S. CURTIS

he had previously read, and the Indian version of American history which he was now learning.[27]

During the next few years, Curtis traveled to the East Coast to present a lecture series on the First Americans at prestigious private clubs, using lantern slides made from his negatives. They were well-attended events — in Washington DC, one of the members in the audience was President Roosevelt. The President saw himself as one of the last frontiersmen, and romantic images of the 'Rough Rider' (as he was popularly called) and the Indians were part of the idea of the American West that he wanted to perpetuate. As a young man, Roosevelt had fought the great chiefs such as the Apache Geronimo and the Comanche Quanah Parker in the Indian wars. Now they rode in the President's inaugural parade. Roosevelt invited Curtis to photograph them, including a picture of Geronimo and five other chiefs on the White House lawn, shivering in the rain after the parade. Roosevelt proclaimed to the public that Curtis's photographs of North American Indians were works of art, as well as valuable historic documents, and he became one of Curtis's most ardent supporters.[28]

After estimating that he had spent about $25,000 of his own money, Curtis sent a proposal letter with an outline for fieldwork among the Indian peoples to the wealthy railroad entrepreneur, J. Pierpont Morgan, in 1906. He wanted to have his photographs published in a work entitled *The North American Indian: . . . Twenty volumes containing fifteen hundred pictures . . . going fully into their history, life, manners, ceremony, legends and mythology.*

According to the original plan, the expense of research and publication was roughly estimated at $1,500,000. Curtis requested and received an interest-free capital loan of $75,000, to cover expenses of $15,000 a year for five years, including $1,800 for motion picture films and payments to Indians for having their pictures taken. The project was to be completed in 1911, and Curtis himself was not to be paid a salary, but would become chief fundraiser and administrator. In return for his investment, Morgan, an avid art collector, was promised twenty-five sets of the work, as well as 500 original prints. Morgan later granted Curtis an additional $60,000 to enable him to continue his fieldwork for another two years, and capitalized a corporation for the publication and sales of *The North American Indian*. Subscribers paid $3,000 for a set consisting of twenty volumes and the same number of portfolios. Additional printings were to be paid for by further sales. When Morgan died in 1913, his son, Jack, became Curtis's supporter. Once Morgan's art collection had been sold, over a ten-year period, the Morgan Bank slowly began to distribute funds to Curtis. But the Pierpont Morgan family fortune only covered printing costs in the forthcoming years, and the struggle for funds was constant.[29]

In addition to the still photographs taken during these years, Curtis and his staff also produced silent films. As early as 1904, he had taken a motion picture camera to the Southwest to film the Navaho Yabachai dance. The next year, he took over six hundred still photographs and filmed the Hopi Snake dance. Curtis's most famous silent film, *In the Land of the Headhunters*, re-created Indian life on the Northwest Coast, and was filmed between 1910 and 1914. The ethnographical data was provided by George Hunt, Kwakiutl informant and photographer for the anthropologist Franz Boas, while the text was based on legends and oral histories. It was dramatically presented, with added romance and violence to appeal to a contemporary audience, and the actors wore specially designed costumes. Curtis produced and directed on behalf of his newly formed Continental Film Company, but in the years to follow the venture was to prove to be a financial failure, possibly due to the more realistic images brought back from the First World War. Yet it had a tremendous impact on future ethnographical films, including Robert Flaherty's 1921 classic, *Nanook of the North*. For the first time, photographers and Indians had made a sortie into the world of film fantasy.[30]

In 1916, the Curtis Studio in Seattle advertised itself as 'The Home of the Curtis Indians', and Curtis began to produce prints which he referred to as 'Curt-Tone'. His technique was a variation of the Orotone process popular at that time, known commercially as 'Goldtone', which referred both to the color and to the special luminous effect achieved by printing the reversed image on glass. The image was then sealed with a viscous mixture of powdered gold pigment and banana oil. The sales catalogue for the studio described the process: 'The new Curt-Tone finish of the Indian studies is most unusual in its depth and lifelike brilliancy ... Mr. Curtis says: The ordinary photographic print, however good, lacks depth and transparency ... but in the new Curt-Tones all the transparency is retained and they are as full of life and sparkle as an opal.'[31]

That same year, Clara Curtis filed for divorce. The years of neglect while her husband was in the field taking pictures and traveling to promote his work on the North American Indians had taken their toll. The divorce, which seems to have been bitter, was finalized in 1919, with Clara receiving everything, including the studio and all its negatives. Curtis's assistants, who may have been family members, apparently destroyed all the glass-plate negatives at this time. From then on, Clara managed the studio with her sister, Sue Phillips Gates, and daughter, Katherine Curtis, selling portraits and goldtones until the studio was sold to Joseph E. Gatchell eight years later.

In 1920 Curtis moved with his photographer daughter, Beth, to Los Angeles to build a new clientele. Since prints from glass-plate negatives appeared at the new studio, duplicate negatives on celluloid must have been made before the originals were destroyed in Seattle. Legally, these would have belonged to Clara, and the sales made from them caused continued bad feelings and financial difficulties.

The second phase of Curtis's life's work was carried on in relative isolation. Publication of *The North American Indian* was in limbo, with volume twelve only finally appearing in 1922, after a six-year lapse. The general public had very little interest in photographs of the North American Indians during the next thirty years. Curtis was ignored by practicing ethnologists at museums and universities, as he had alienated most of them by his independence and lack of interest in their work. His colleagues and powerful patrons had either retired or died and he lost their emotional and financial support. During this dark period, he turned, once again, to fantasy—the movies.

Curtis's first assignment in the Hollywood of the 1920s was biblical research for Cecil B. DeMille's *Ten Commandments*. He later served as stills photographer and cameraman for the film, and for DeMille's *Adam's Rib* and *King of Kings*. In 1936, he went to South Dakota to work on the *The Plainsman*. During this period, he received an offer from anthropologists Pliny Earl Goddard and Franz Boas to purchase a portion of *In the Land of the Headhunters*, for the American Museum of Natural History. Goddard and Boaz wanted only the ethnographic footage of house posts and a canoe made by the Kwakiutl peoples under George Hunt's direction. The cost of these sequences had represented most of Curtis's budget for the film.

Curtis had lost $75,000 in the making of *In the Land of the Headhunters*. Now he was working for someone who specialized in entertainment, and who spent in a few months more than Curtis had spent in his entire thirty years of ethnographic work among the Indians.

Whatever he might have thought about the museum's request for his film, Curtis needed money. He sold the uncut master negative and print for $1,500, relinquishing all rights to his film.[32]

In 1930, volumes nineteen and twenty of *The North American Indian* were finally published. The introduction to the last volume gratefully acknowledged the contribution of the Morgan family, who by that time had spent about $400,000 on the project. Curtis wrote:

'Great is the satisfaction the writer enjoys when he can at last say to all those whose faith has been unbounded, it is finished.'[33]

Curtis died of a heart attack on 19 October 1952, at the home of his daughter, Beth Curtis Magnuson. The *New York Times* gave him a seventy-six word obituary, in which he was listed as an authority on the history of the North American Indian. It was also noted that he was known as a photographer.

Curtis's photographic work on the North American Indians spanned thirty years, from 1900 to 1930, covered approximately eighty tribes, and resulted in approximately forty thousand images. He also wrote four books, supervised sixteen others and made more than ten thousand records of Indian speech and music—a staggering amount in one lifetime. In 1948, the Washington Historical Society inherited fifteen volumes and fifteen portfolios of pictures of *The North American Indian*. Original copper gravure plates were rediscovered in the basement of the Lauriat bookshop in New York City in 1977, and reprinting has made some images available to the general public. Curtis's work is found in numerous private and museum collections, but forty years after his death, the true value of this magnum opus has yet to be fully realized.

The Pictorialists of the American West followed the old trails but with a new freedom to photograph in a relatively peaceful atmosphere. They were free from wars, that is, but instead were surrounded by throngs of anthropologists, university researchers and tourists, who flocked on the new railroads to travel to Indian sites. Like the frontier photographers before them, the Pictorialists carried large-format glass-plate view cameras and not the Kodak box camera of the amateur.

Reed, Dixon and Curtis were professional photographers with a serious purpose in mind. They thought of themselves as visual historians, belonging both to the scientific and artistic communities. As a scientific pursuit, they wanted to conduct ethnographic studies, and record the traditional Indian ways of life before they vanished completely. Idealistically, they ventured out to discover the 'noble savage' of myth. Instead, they found disheartened peoples, living in despair on reservations. Realism made bad photographs, and the Pictorialists believed that their artistic skills could make what they had found beautiful again. As artists, they had imagination and a respect for their subjects, using the camera as an instrument of creative expression, just as a painter uses his brush.

Photography is also a story-telling medium. Each picture automatically implies a time before and after its taking. The world depicted in the photograph may never actually have been, and we may never know the real story. But we know that reality existed before and will go on after the picture is taken. Moreover, the making of a photograph is as much a decision about what to leave out, as it is a selection of what is kept in. The Pictorialists did not intend to delude the viewer by altering or excluding elements of the image—rather, they wanted to take their audience back to a vanished world and remind them of what had been destroyed; to give back to the Indians what had been taken away. They looked to their subjects for those ethnographic and artistic elements that would lend themselves to this.

And so began a complex conspiracy between the photographers and the North American Indians. Together, they produced an idealized vision that satisfied both their needs, with both parties participating in re-creating the history of an entire nation. The West became the symbol of America's romantic youth; the Indians themselves, the symbol of ancient wisdom and hope for the future.

The writing of this book is our endeavor to illustrate the tremendous impact of the cultural clash between the aboriginal population and the newcomers to the American West which brought about this situation, as recorded by its master photographers. Our purpose in publishing these images is to give back to the North American Indians a part of their own history. The pictures should make us aware of the missing voice of the Indian in our history books. They convey that these peoples were and are of a place, and that they were and are of a time—the time of the ancestors before, and the time of the generations who will come after. They have not and will not vanish. They are brave, resilient and dignified peoples, they are the first Americans, and belong to the overall culture of the country, as well as to their own. We hope by this publication, and others like it, that this message will be conveyed.

'We are here now, have been here for thousands of years, and we will always be here. We have fooled them all!'

George Horse Capture, Gros Ventre

*Not a Real Woman with horse
and travois in Glacier National
Park, 1915.*
ROLAND REED

*'The Council'
Blackfoot Indians in Glacier
National Park, 1915.*
ROLAND REED

ABOVE
Blackfoot chief in full headdress. An undated portrait.
ROLAND REED

RIGHT
Curley Bear, a Blackfoot, 1915.
ROLAND REED

'Echo's Call'
Undated study of a Blackfoot
camp.
ROLAND REED

'Song of the Canyon'
Blackfoot, undated.
ROLAND REED

Daisy Norris
ROLAND REED

'The Pottery Maker'
This photograph won a gold
medal at the Panama–Pacific
Exposition in San Francisco in
1915.
ROLAND REED

'Stringing the Bow'
A Navaho Indian, photographed
between 1913 and 1915.
ROLAND REED

*Undated study of one of the
ancient cliff dwellings of the
Anasazi culture of the Southwest.*
ROLAND REED

LEFT
A view of the Casa Blanca ruins.
ROLAND REED

ABOVE
'Alone with the Past'
Navaho Indians looking at the
Casa Blanca ruins of the ancient
Anasazi culture (circa AD 600–
1300) in the Canyon de Chelley,
New Mexico.
ROLAND REED

'Shepherd of the Hills', 1915.
Portrait of a Navaho Indian of
the Southwest, called Many
Coats.
ROLAND REED

Hopi Walpi pueblo, Arizona,
1915.
ROLAND REED

Emma, a Kickapoo, draped in an American flag to symbolize the patriotism of the North American Indians. Photographed for the Wanamaker Expedition of Citizenship of 1913.
Joseph Kossuth Dixon

Haskayelthnaga, a Navaho. This picture was exhibited at the Panama–Pacific Exposition, San Francisco, in 1915. Taken on the Wanamaker Expedition of Citizenship, 1913.
JOSEPH KOSSUTH DIXON

LEFT
Chief Red Cloud, an Oglala Sioux, photographed during the
Wanamaker Expedition of Citizenship, 1913.
JOSEPH KOSSUTH DIXON

ABOVE
Holding Eagle, of the Gros Ventre tribe. Photographed during the
Wanamaker Expedition of Citizenship, 1913.
JOSEPH KOSSUTH DIXON

FAR LEFT
'Sunset of a Dying Race', a
Wanamaker Expedition
photograph.
JOSEPH KOSSUTH DIXON

LEFT
'Singing to the Spirits', another
photograph from the Wanamaker
Expeditions.
JOSEPH KOSSUTH DIXON

LEFT
'At the Bath'
JOSEPH KOSSUTH DIXON

RIGHT
Mrs Wolf Plume, a Blackfoot,
photographed on a Wanamaker
Expedition.
JOSEPH KOSSUTH DIXON

'The Last Outpost'
JOSEPH KOSSUTH DIXON

A Blackfoot tipi, photographed on one of the Wanamaker Expeditions.
JOSEPH KOSSUTH DIXON

'Gathering Buffalo Berries'
JOSEPH KOSSUTH DIXON

LEFT
'Climbing the Western Slope'
JOSEPH KOSSUTH DIXON

RIGHT
'Stirring the Pot'
JOSEPH KOSSUTH DIXON

BELOW
'The Bathers'
JOSEPH KOSSUTH DIXON

ABOVE LEFT
Takes Five, a Crow, photographed at the Valley of the Little Bighorn, Montana, in 1909. An illustration from The Vanishing Race.
JOSEPH KOSSUTH DIXON

BELOW LEFT
Chief Umapine of the Cayuse, a portrait taken for The Vanishing Race *at the Valley of the Little Bighorn, Montana, 1909.*
JOSEPH KOSSUTH DIXON

ABOVE RIGHT
Chief Bear Ghost, Crow/Creek/Sioux, photographed for The Vanishing Race. *Valley of the Little Bighorn, Montana, 1909.*
JOSEPH KOSSUTH DIXON

OPPOSITE
Chief Tin-Tin-Meetsa, Umatilla, an illustration for The Vanishing Race. *Valley of the Little Bighorn, Montana, 1909.*
JOSEPH KOSSUTH DIXON

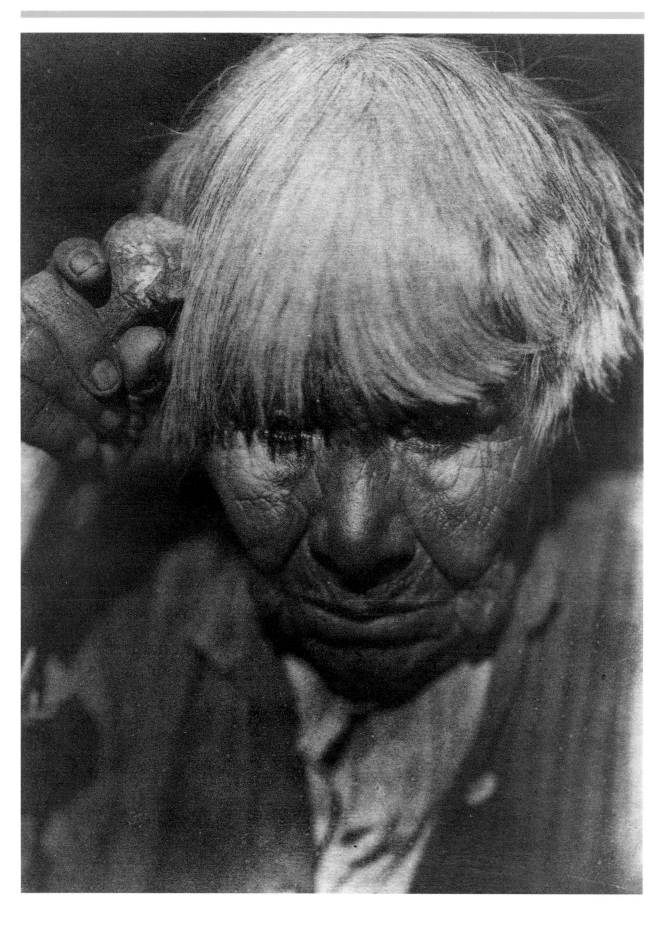

ABOVE

'Old Woman in Mourning—Yuki' EDWARD S. CURTIS

RIGHT

Chief Red Cloud of the Oglala Sioux, circa 1905. EDWARD S. CURTIS

'An Assiniboin Camp'
EDWARD S. CURTIS

'A Heavy Load', Sioux. Women
performed the heavy work of the
camp.
EDWARD S. CURTIS

'The Blanket Weaver', Navaho.
Taken in summer, when the
looms were erected outdoors.
EDWARD S. CURTIS

'On the Little Bighorn',
Montana. This photograph was
taken circa 1908, a short
distance from where Crow scouts
led General George Armstrong
Custer and the US 7th Cavalry
to fight the Sioux at the famous
Battle of the Little Bighorn in
1876.
EDWARD S. CURTIS

Slow Bull, an Oglala Sioux.
EDWARD S. CURTIS

Horse Capture, an Atsina. EDWARD S. CURTIS

'Spokan Man'   EDWARD S. CURTIS

LEFT

'Nespilim Girl'   EDWARD S. CURTIS

ABOVE

'Quilcene Boy', from Hoods Canal, Washington Territory.   EDWARD S. CURTIS

'*Medicine Bags*' EDWARD S. CURTIS

'Hano Potter', a portrait of the Tewa potter, Serpent Who Has No Tooth (Nampeyo). Hano pueblo, Arizona. EDWARD S. CURTIS

Navaho man portraying Nayenezgoni (Slayer of the Alien Powers) of Yabachai, the Night Chant ceremony.   EDWARD S. CURTIS

'The Pledger', Piegan.   EDWARD S. CURTIS

*Two Whistles, Apsaroke
(Crow).*
EDWARD S. CURTIS

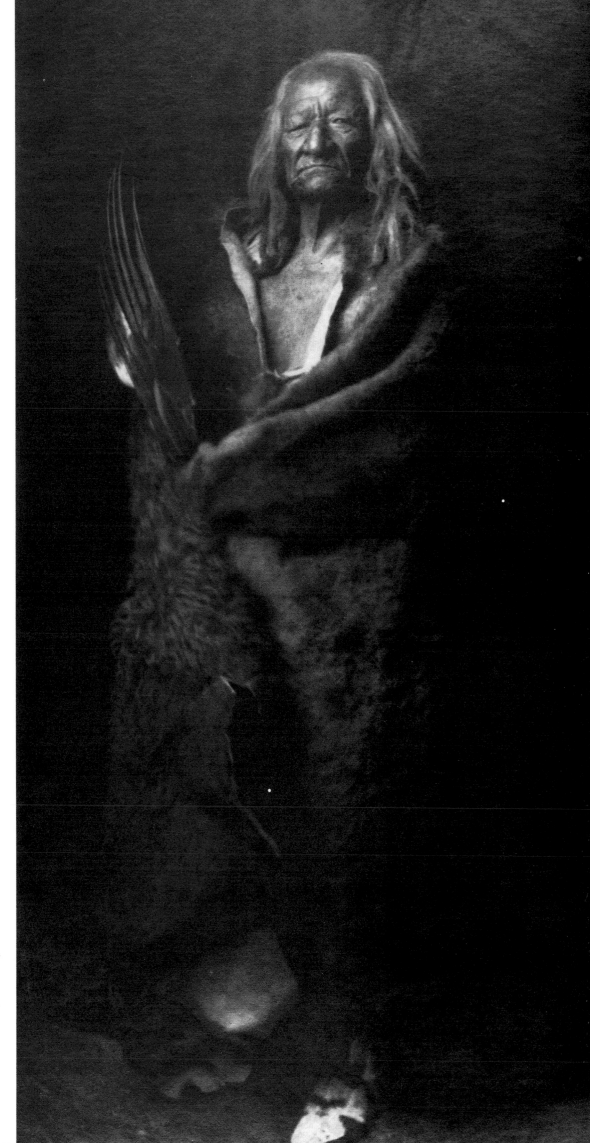

Black Eagle, an Assiniboin.
EDWARD S. CURTIS

'Evening on Puget Sound'
This photograph, which was
taken near Seattle, won a bronze
medal at the National
Photographers' Convention in
Chautaugqua, New York, in
1896, for 'excellence in posing,
lighting and tone'.
EDWARD S. CURTIS

ABOVE
'Dancing to Restore the Moon',
Quagyuhl (Kwakiutl), 1901. The
Kwakiutl believed that an eclipse
resulted from a sky creature's
attempt to swallow the moon. The
people are dancing round a
smoldering fire of old clothing and
hair, the stench of which rises
into the creature's realm and
causes him to sneeze, and thus
disgorge the moon.
EDWARD S. CURTIS

RIGHT
'Fire Drill', Koskimo.
EDWARD S. CURTIS

'Watching the Dancers', Hopi maidens on a rooftop of Walpi pueblo, Arizona, looking down into the Plaza.　　EDWARD S. CURTIS

Footnotes

KEY TO ABBREVIATIONS

GPO: Government Printing Office
NARA: National Archives and Records Administration
SIA: Smithsonian Institution Archives
SI–AR: Smithsonian Institution – Annual Report
SIA–RU: Smithsonian Institution Archives – Record Unit
SINAA: Smithsonian Institution National Anthropological Archives
SINAA–BAE: Smithsonian Institution National Anthropological Archives –
                          Bureau of American Ethnology

Works identified by the author's name only are cited in full in the
Bibliography.

INTRODUCTION

1   Justice Joseph Story, 'Discourse, Pronounced at the Request of the Essex Historical Society, Sept. 18, 1828, in Commemoration of the First Settlement of Salem, Mass.'. Quoted in Dippie, (1982): 1
2   *Philadelphia Photographer*, 1866, III, 35: 339
3   Ibid., 36: 371
4   Review of Colonel Richard Irving Dodge, 'Our Wild Indians'. SINAA, MS 4605: 116 (apparently clipped from *Puck's Library*, 1888, XVIII, 22)
5   William Morris (ed.), *The American Heritage Dictionary of the English Language*, Houghton Mifflin Company, Boston, 1981
6   Horse Capture: 60
7   Current and Current: 226
8   Frederick Monsen, 'Picturing Indians with the Camera', *Photo-Era*, 1910, XXV:165–78. Quoted in Mitchell, Lee Clark: 111
9   Fleming and Luskey: 214
10 Dippie (1982): 25

CHAPTER 1

1   Donaldson: 745
2   Mitchell, Lee Clark: 97
3   Catlin, vol. I: 19 (1973 reprint: ix)
4   Ibid.: 36 (1973 reprint: 16)
5   Mitchell, Lee Clark: 100
6   DeVoto: 391–2
7   Catlin, vol. I: 19 (1973 reprint: xii)
8   Taylor: 40
9   Historical Society of New Mexico, item no. 0407. Quoted in Taylor: 41–2
10 Horan: 23
11 Horan: 61
12 Viola (1976): 20
13 Viola (1976): 21
14 Viola (1974): 245
15 Viola (1974): 248

16 Horan: 91
17 *Philadelphia American Saturday Courier*, 2 April 1842
18 McDermott: 2
19 Mitchell, Lee Clark: 123–4
20 Eastman (1962 reprint): xvi
21 McDermott: 17
22 Joseph Henry to James Denver, 21 February 1859. NARA, Indian Affairs, Record Group 75, letters received (misc.)
23 McClees circular in SINAA, W. W. Turner papers, acc. 76–112
24 Blackmore diary XVI, 1868: 17. History Library, Museum of New Mexico, William Blackmore Collection, box 8, item 0070
25 Jackson (1874), preface
26 Blackmore to Hayden, 4 March 1875. NARA, Correspondence of the US Geological Survey, microfilm 623, roll 16
27 Jackson (1877): iv

CHAPTER 2

1   Hamilton: 101
2   Mitchell, Lynn Marie: 101
3   Hamilton: 12
4   Mitchell, Lynn Marie: 101
5   Roosa: 389
6   Statement by Charley Eads. Quoted in Hamilton: 11
7   Roosa: 389
8   Hamilton: 10
9   Anderson, John Alvin: (introduction)
10 Hamilton: 11
11 Mitchell, Lynn Marie: 102
12 Hamilton: 12
13 Marion Pond Harrison, personal letter to Wendy Cunkle, 31 May 1978. Quoted in Cunkle: 71
14 Wyatt (1989): 13. Wyatt points out newspaper accounts differ as to which of the partners actually bought out Landerking, although it appears

likely that it was Winter.
15 Wyatt (1989): 24
16 Cunkle–Jorgenson interview, 31 January 1977. Quoted in Cunkle: 73
17 Wyatt (1989): 36
18 John D. Ward of the Alaska Native Brotherhood, personal letter, 7 January 1928. Quoted in Cunkle: 74
19 Drucker: 165
20 Haycox: 40
21 *Daily Alaska Empire*, 23 November 1945: 5. Quoted in Cunkle: 14
22 Wyatt (1989): 14
23 Wyatt (1989): 16
24 George Wharton James, *Camera Craft*, November 1901. Quoted in Webb and Weinstein: 14
25 Maurer: 4
26 Maurer: 6
27 Maurer: 6
28 Arreola: 12
29 Arreola: 12
30 Webb and Weinstein: 14
31 Patrick T. Houlihan, 'Director's View: George Wharton James', *Masterkey*, 1986, LX, 1: 2–3
32 Arreola: 13
33 Arreola: 14
34 *The New York Times*, 27 January 1906
35 Arreola: 17
36 James: 150 and 153
37 Cortes: 25
38 Statement by Charles Wagner, a French government minister. Quoted in Cortes: 25
39 Casagrande and Bourne: 13
40 Ritzenthaler and Johnson: 62
41 Casagrande and Bourne: 4
42 Matteson to William H. Holmes, 4 July 1908. SINAA–BAE, letters received
43 Casagrande and Bourne: 230
44 Casagrande and Bourne: 10
45 Matteson to William H. Holmes, 4 July 1908. SINAA–BAE, letters received
46 Webb and Weinstein: 13–14
47 Bourne: 13
48 Matteson: 93–4
49 Matteson: 97
50 Matteson: 99
51 Horse Capture: 70
52 Matteson to William H. Holmes, 1 July 1908. SINAA–BAE, letters received
53 Letter from Roosevelt to Matteson. Quoted in Casagrande and Bourne: 32
54 Matteson to William H.

Holmes, 10 January 1908. SINAA–BAE, letters received
55 Casagrande and Bourne: 33
56 Horse Capture: 71
57 Horse Capture: 71

CHAPTER 3

1   *Tallis's History and Description of Crystal Palace*, John Tallis Inc., New York, 1851, I: 119 and II: 192. SIA
2   SINAA vertical file: 'Bonaparte'
3   John Carter (Nebraska State Historical Society), personal letter to Judith Lynn Luskey, 15 May 1992
4   SINAA vertical file: 'Bonaparte'
5   *New York Times*, 14 April 1924 and *Washington Post*, 14 April 1924
6   Anonymous MS, 'World's Fairs' or Large Expositions, 1975(?). SIA
7   SINAA, MS 4410 (John K. Hillers's diaries for 1872–3 and 1875)
8   SI–AR, 1876: 57
9   SI–AR, 1894: 605
10 SIA Earll to Good RU70, box 39, 1892
11 SIA–RU70, box 31: 134
12 SIA–RU70, box 31: 137
13 SINAA–BAE, 1893–4: xci
14 SI–AR, 1894
15 Royal Sutton, *The Face of Courage: The Rinehart Collection of Indian Photographs*, The Old Army Press, Fort Collins, Colo., 1972: (1)
16 James Mooney, 'The Indian Congress at Omaha', *American Anthropologist*, 1899, I, 1: 127
17 Bratley: 26
18 Sutton, op. cit.: 5
19 Frank A. Rinehart, *Rinehart's Indians*, Rinehart, Omaha, 1899: 1
20 Robert Bigart and Clarence Woodcock, 'The Trans-Mississippi Exposition of the Flathead Delegation', *Montana, The Magazine of Western History*, 1979, XXIX, 4: 16–17
21 Herbert Welsh to Frances E. Leupp and W. B. Allen, 3 December 1897. Indian Rights Association Papers, H.S.P.
22 Robert Bigart and Clarence Woodcock, op. cit.: 19
23 James Mooney to John Wesley Powell, 20 October 1898. SINAA–BAE, letters received
24 Robert Bigart and Clarence Woodcock, op. cit.: 15
25 Joslyn Art Museum, Omaha, Nebraska (exposition booklet)
26 Robert Bigart and Clarence Woodcock, op. cit.: 22

27 James Mooney, op. cit.: 147
28 James Mooney to John Wesley Powell, 20 October 1898. SINAA–BAE, letters received
29 Robert Bigart and Clarence Woodcock, op. cit.: 23
30 SI–AR, 1905
31 *Gould's City and Business Directory of St Louis*, Gould, St Louis, 1903
32 Duane Sneddecker (Missouri Historical Society), personal communication to Judith Lynn Luskey
33 Ibid.

CHAPTER 4
1 Current and Current: 227
2 Johnston: 44–57
3 Johnston: 44–57
4 Johnston: 49
5 Ruby: 48–62
6 Johnston: 56
7 Kramer Gallery and Studio (1981): 1–2
8 Joseph Kossuth Dixon, *The Vanishing Race: The Last Great Indian Council*, Doubleday, Page & Company, Garden City, New York, 1913: 93
9 Ibid.: 208
10 Reynolds: 2
11 Joseph Kossuth Dixon, op. cit. (foreword by Rodman Wanamaker)
12 Ibid.: v
13 Reynolds
14 Davis: 21
15 Davis: 17–19
16 Davis: 21
17 Davis: 29
18 Davis: 23
19 Davis: 23
20 Davis: 25
21 Davis: 28
22 Davis: 31
23 Davis: 48 and 52
24 Davis: 54 and 64
25 Davis: 37 and 55
26 Davis: 37
27 Davis: 52
28 Davis: 40
29 Davis: 64
30 Lyman: 37–60
31 Kirlin: 100
32 Davis: 69–72
33 Davis: 74–5

Picture Credits

2–3 SINAA
8 SINAA
10 SINAA
12 SINAA
14 SINAA
15 *above* SINAA
15 *below* SINAA
16 SINAA
23 SIL
24 Smithsonian Institution–Nat. Museum of American Art 1985.66.1
25 SINAA
26 *above* SINAA
27 SINAA
28 SINAA
30 NSHS, neg. no. A547–70A
32 NSHS, neg. no. A547–88F
34–5 ASL, neg. no. 87–001 and 87–002
38 SINAA
42 NSHS, neg. no. A547–165A
43 NSHS, neg. no. A547–6P
44 NSHS, neg. no. A547–1
45 NSHS, neg. no. A547–27P
46 NSHS, neg. no. A547–5P
47 NSHS, neg. no. A547–69P
48 NSHS, neg. no. A547–67P
49 NSHS, neg. no. A547–228
50–51 ASL, neg. no. 87–043
52 ASL, neg. no. 87–297
53 ASL, neg. no. 87–007
56 ASL, neg. no. 87–020
57 *above* ASL, neg. no. 87–296
57 *below* ASL, neg. no. 87–037
58 ASL, neg. no. 87–303
59 ASL, neg. no. 87–070
60 SINAA
61 SINAA
62 *above* SINAA
62 *below* SINAA

63 SINAA
64–5 SINAA
66 SINAA
67 SINAA
68 *above* MPM, neg. no. 44,276
68 *below* MPM, neg. no. 43,781
69 SINAA
70 MPM, neg. no. 43,922
71 MPM, neg. no. 112,055
72 *above* SINAA
72 *below* MPM, neg. no. 44,775
73 MPM, neg. no. 44,610
74 MPM, neg. no. 44,480
75 MPM, neg. no. 44,509
76 SINAA
78 SINAA
82 SINAA
85 SINAA
86 SINAA
87 SINAA
88 SINAA
89 SINAA
90 SINAA
91 SINAA
92 MHS, Gerhard, no. WF 1063
93 SINAA
94 SINAA
95 SINAA
96 SINAA
97 MHS, Gerhard, no. WF 1064
98 SIL
101 By permission of the Kramer Gallery and Studio, St Paul, Minnesota – *Into the Wilderness*
102 SINAA
104 no. 316631 (Photo: Wanamaker Collection – President Wilson's Speech on Phonograph). Courtesy Department Library Services, American Museum of Natural

History
109 SIL; Copyright 1899, published 1913
114 SIL
118 By permission of the Kramer Gallery and Studio, St Paul, Minnesota – *The Council*
119 By permission of the Kramer Gallery and Studio, St Paul, Minnesota – *Woman with Travois*
120 SINAA
121 By permission of the Kramer Gallery and Studio, St Paul, Minnesota – *Curley Bear*
122–3 SINAA
124 By permission of the Kramer Gallery and Studio, St Paul, Minnesota – *Echo's Call*
125 SINAA
126 By permission of the Kramer Gallery and Studio, St Paul, Minnesota – *The Pottery Maker*
127 By permission of the Kramer Gallery and Studio, St Paul, Minnesota – *Stringing the Bow*
128–9 By permission of the Kramer Gallery and Studio, St Paul, Minnesota – *Ancient Dwellings*
130 By permission of the Kramer Gallery and Studio, St Paul, Minnesota – *Casa Blanca*
131 By permission of the Kramer Gallery and Studio, St Paul, Minnesota – *Alone with the Past*
132 By permission of the Kramer Gallery and Studio, St Paul, Minnesota – *Shepherd of the Hills*
133 By permission of the Kramer Gallery and Studio, St Paul, Minnesota – *Walpi Pueblo*
134 no. 316978 (Photo: Wanamaker Collection – Emma Kickapoo). Courtesy Department Library Services, American Museum of Natural History
135 no. 316423 (Photo: Wanamaker Collection – Navajo Boy). Courtesy Department Library

Services, American Museum of Natural History
136 no. 316461 (Photo: Wanamaker Collection – Oglala Sioux, Jack Red Cloud). Courtesy Department Library Services, American Museum of Natural History
137 no. 316833 (Photo: Wanamaker Collection – Gros Ventre, Holding Eagle). Courtesy Department Library Services, American Museum of Natural History
138 SINAA
139 SINAA
140 SINAA
141 SINAA
142 SINAA
143 *above* SINAA
143 *below* SINAA
144 *above* SINAA
144 *below* SINAA
145 SINAA
146 *above left* SINAA
146 *above right* SINAA
146 *below* SINAA
147 SINAA
148 SIL
149 SIL
150–1 SIL
152 SIL
153 SIL
154 SIL
155 SIL
156 SIL
157 SIL
158 SIL
159 SIL
160 SIL
161 SIL
162 SIL
163 SIL
164 SIL
165 SIL
166–7 SIL
168 SIL
169 SIL
170 SIL

Bibliography

Anderson, John Alvin, *Among the Sioux*, J. A. Anderson, Rosebud Agency, S. Dak., 1896

Anderson, Myrtle Miller, *Sioux Memory Gems*, Chicago, 1929

Arreola, Paul R., 'George Wharton James and the Indians', *Masterkey*, 1986, LX, 1: 11–18

Berkhofer, Robert F., Jr., *The White Man's Indian*, Alfred A. Knopf, New York, 1978

—— 'White Conceptions of Indians', *Handbook of North American Indians: History of Indian–White Relations*, Smithsonian Institution Press, Washington DC, 1988, IV: 522–47

Bigart, Robert, and Woodcock, Clarence, 'The Trans-Mississippi Exposition of the Flathead Delegation', *Montana, The Magazine of Western History*, 1979, XXIX, 4: 14–23

Bourdon, Roger J., *George Wharton James, Interpreter of the Southwest*, University of California at Los Angeles, 1966 (PhD diss.)

Bourne, Phillips M., 'Matteson as Photographer', *The Science Museum of Minnesota, Encounters*, 1982, V, 6: 12–13

Bratley, J[esse] H[astings], 'Teaching Indians of the Plains', in Reutter, Winifred (comp.), *Dakota Days*, Argus Printers, Stickney, S. Dak., 1962: 24–9

Casagrande, Louis B., and Barbre, Joy, 'Side Trips: The Illustrated Adventures of Sumner Matteson', *The Science Museum of Minnesota, Encounters*, 1982, V, 6: 6–9

Casagrande, Louis B., and Bourne, Phillips, *Side Trips: The Photography of Sumner W. Matteson, 1898–1908*, Milwaukee Public Museum and Science Museum of Minnesota, 1983

Catlin, George, *Letters and Notes on the Manners, Customs and Conditions of the North American Indians Written During Eight Years Travel (1832–1839) Amongst the Wildest Tribes of Indians in North America*, two vols, David Bogue, London, 1844. Reprinted (with an introduction by Marjorie Halpin) Dover Publications, Inc., New York, 1973

Cortes, Enrique, 'Advocate for the Golden State: George Wharton James in California', *Masterkey*, 1986, LX, 1: 19–25

Cunkle, Wendy, *Winter and Pond: Pioneer Photographers in Alaska*, San Francisco State University, 1979 (MA thesis)

Current, Karen, and Current, William R., *Photography and the Old West*, Harry N. Abrams Inc., New York/The Amon Carter Museum of Western Art, Fort Worth, Texas, 1978

Curtis, Edward S., *The North American Indian: Being a Series of Volumes Picturing and Describing the Indians of the United States, and Alaska*, twenty vols, Harvard University Press, Cambridge, Mass., 1907–30

Davis, Barbara A., *Edward S. Curtis: The Life and Times of a Shadow Catcher*, Chronicle Books, San Francisco, 1985

DeVoto, Bernard, *Across the Wide Missouri*, Houghton Mifflin Company, Boston, 1947

Dippie, Brian W., *The Vanishing American: White Attitudes and U.S. Indian Policy*, Wesleyan University Press, Middletown, Conn., 1982

—— *Catlin and His Contemporaries: The Politics of Patronage*, University of Nebraska Press, Lincoln, Nebr., 1990

Doll, Don, and Alinder, Jim (eds), *Crying for a Vision: A Rosebud Sioux Trilogy, 1886–1976. Photographs by John A. Anderson, Eugene Buechel, Don Doll*, Morgan and Morgan, Dobbs Ferry, NY, 1976

Donaldson, Thomas, 'The George Catlin Indian Gallery in the United States National Museum (Smithsonian Institution) with Memoir and Statistics', SI–AR 1885, GPO, Washington DC, 1887, part II: 3–939

Drucker, Philip, 'The Native Brotherhoods: Modern Intertribal Organizations on the Northwest Coast', *Bureau of American Ethnology Bulletin 168*, GPO, Washington DC, 1958

Dyck, Paul, *Brule: The Sioux People of the Rosebud*, Northland Press, Flagstaff, Ariz., 1971

Eastman, Mary, *Dahcotah; or, Life and Legends of the Sioux Around Fort Snelling*, Wiley, New York, 1849. Reprinted Ross and Haines, Minneapolis, 1962

Ewers, John Canfield, 'An Anthropologist Looks at Early Pictures of North American Indians', *New York Historical Society Quarterly Bulletin*, 1949, XXXII, 4: 223–34

—— 'George Catlin, Painter of Indians and the West', *SI–AR 1955*, Smithsonian Institution Press, Washington DC, 1956

Farr, William E., *The Reservation Blackfeet, 1882–1945: A Photographic History of Cultural Survival*, University of Washington Press, Seattle, 1984

Fleming, Paula Richardson, 'Indianer på glasplåt — traditionen att fotografera indianer', in Jacobson, Claes-Håkan, *Rosebud Sioux: Ett Folk i Förvandling*, Forlag C. H. Jacobson Produktion AB, Stockholm, 1989: 60–82

Fleming, Paula Richardson, and Luskey, Judith, *The North American Indians in Early Photographs*, Harper & Row, New York, 1986. Reprinted Dorset Press, New York, 1992

Hamilton, Henry W., and Tyree, Jean, *The Sioux of the Rosebud: A History in Pictures*, University of Oklahoma Press, Norman, Okla., 1971

Haycox, Stephen, 'Alaskan Native Brotherhood Conventions: Sites and Grand Officers, 1912–1959', *Alaska History*, 1989, IV, 2: 39–46

Horan, James D., *The McKenney–Hall Portrait Gallery of American Indians*, Crown Publishing Group, New York, 1972

Horse Capture, George, 'The Camera Eye of Sumner Matteson', *Montana, The Magazine of Western History*, 1977, XXVII, 3: 48–61

Jackson, William Henry, *Descriptive Catalogue of the Photographs of the United States Geological Survey of the Territories for the Years 1869 to 1873 Inclusive*, US Department of the Interior Miscellaneous Publications no. 5 (first edition only), GPO, Washington DC, 1874

—— *Descriptive Catalogue of Photographs of North American Indians*, US Department of the Interior Miscellaneous Publications no. 9, GPO, Washington DC, 1877

Jacobson, Claes-Håkan, *Rosebud Sioux: Ett Folk i Förvandling*, Forlag C. H. Jacobson Produktion AB, Stockholm, 1989

James, George W[harton], 'Palomas Apaches and Their Baskets', *Sunset*, 1903, XI: 146–53

'John Alvin Anderson, Frontier Photographer', *Nebraska History*, 1970, LI, 4: 469–8

Johnston, Patricia Condon, 'The Indian Photographs of Roland Reed', *The American West*, 1978, XV, 2: 44–57

Kirlin, Raymond H., and Womack, Darrel. '"Curt-Tones"; The Goldtones of Edward S. Curtis', *Hobbies, The Magazine for Collectors*, 1981, June: 100–2

Kramer Gallery and Studio, *Images of the Southwest: Photographs of the American Indian. Roland Reed, Photographer, 1864–1934*, Kramer Gallery, St Paul, Minn., n.d.

—— *Images of the Plains: Piegan Views I, Photographs of the American Indian. Roland Reed, Photographer, 1864–1934*, Kramer Gallery, St Paul, Minn., n.d.

Lyman, Christopher, *The Vanishing Race and Other Illusions: Photographs of Indians by Edward S. Curtis*, Smithsonian Institution Press, Washington DC, 1982. See also Holm, Bill, review of the above work, *American Indian Art Magazine*, 1983, VIII, 3: 68–73

Matteson, Sumner W., 'The Fourth of July Celebration at Fort Belknap', *Pacific Monthly*, 1906, XVI, 1: 93–103

Maurer, Stephen G., 'In the Heart of the Great Freedom: George Wharton James and the Desert Southwest', *Masterkey*, 1986, LX, 1: 4–10

McDermott, John Francis, *The Art of Seth Eastman*, Smithsonian Institution Press, Washington DC, 1956

McKenney, Thomas Loraine, and Hall, James, *History of the Indian Tribes of North America, with Biographical Sketches and Anecdotes of the Principal Chiefs. Embellished with One Hundred and Twenty Portraits, from the Indian Gallery in the Department of War, at Washington*, D. Rice and J. G. Clark, Philadelphia, 1836–44. (Also J. T. Bowen, Philadelphia, 1848–50; D. Rice and A. N. Hart, Philadelphia, 1858; Rice, Rutter, Philadelphia, 1868; D. Rice and Co., Philadelphia, 187?)

Mitchell, Lee Clark, *Witness to a Vanishing America: The Nineteenth-Century Response*, Princeton University Press, Princeton, 1981

Mitchell, Lynn Marie, *Shadow Catchers on the Great Plains: Four Frontier Photographers of American Indians*, University of Oklahoma, 1987 (MA thesis)

—— 'William Richard Cross, Photographer on the Nebraska–South Dakota Frontier', *South Dakota History*, 1990, XX, 2: 81–95

Monsen, Frederick, 'Pictures of Indians with the Camera', *Photo-Era*, 1910, XXV: 165–78

Photographs of the Principal Chiefs of the North American Indians, taken when they have Visited Washington as Deputations from their Tribes, Trustees of the Blackmore Museum, Salisbury, England, 1865

Reynolds, Charles, 'Photographs from the Dixon/Wanamaker Expedition, 1913', *Infinity: The American Society of Magazine Photographers' Trade Journal*, 1971: 1–30

Rinehart, Frank A., *Rinehart's Prints of American Indians*, Frank A. Rinehart, Omaha, Neb., 1900

Ritzenthaler, Robert E., and Johnson, Leo, 'The Artistry of Sumner W. Matteson', *American Indian Art Magazine*, 1979, V, 1: 61–7

Roosa, Alma Carlson, 'Homesteading in the 1880's: The Anderson–Carlson Families of Cherry County', *Nebraska History*, 1972, LVIII, 3: 371–94

Ruby, Jay, 'Photographs of the Piegan by Roland Reed', *Studies in Visual Communication*, 1981, VII, 1: 48–62

Schoolcraft, Henry Rowe, *Historical and Statistical Information Respecting the History, Condition, and Prospects of the Indian Tribes of the United States; collected and prepared under the direction of the Bureau of Indian Affairs per act of Congress of March 3rd 1847*, six vols, Lippincott, Grambo & Co., Philadelphia, 1851–7

Schultz, James Willard, *Blackfeet Tales of Glacier National Park*, Houghton Mifflin Company, Boston, 1916

[Shindler, Antonio Zeno,] 'Photographic Portraits of North American Indians in the Gallery of the Smithsonian Institution', 1867 (1869), *Smithsonian Miscellaneous Collection*, 1876, XIV, 216

Stedman, Raymond William, *Shadows of the Indian: Stereotypes in American Culture*, University of Oklahoma Press, Norman, Okla., 1982

Taft, Robert, *Photography and the American Scene: A Social History, 1839–1889*, Macmillan Co., New York, 1938. Reprinted Dover Publications, Inc., New York, 1964

Taylor, Colin, '"Ho, for the Great West!", Indians and Buffalo, Exploration and George Catlin: The West of William Blackmore', in Johnson, Barry C. (ed.), *'Ho, for the Great West!' and Other Papers to Mark the 25th Anniversary of the English Westerners' Society*, London (for the English Westerners' Society), 1980: 9–49

Truettner, William H., *A Study of Catlin's Indian Gallery*, Smithsonian Institution Press, Washington DC, 1979

Viola, Herman, *Thomas L. McKenney; Architect of America's Early Indian Policy, 1816–1830*, The Swallow Press, Inc., Chicago, 1974

—— *The Indian Legacy of Charles Bird King*, Smithsonian Institution Press, Washington DC, 1976

Webb, William, and Weinstein, Robert A., *Dwellers at the Source: Southwestern Indian Photographs of A. C. Vroman, 1895–1904*, University of New Mexico Press, Albuquerque, N. Mex., 1973

Wyatt, Victoria, *Images from the Inside Passage: An Alaskan Portrait by Winter and Pond*, University of Washington Press, Seattle, 1989

—— 'Interpreting the Balance of Power: A Case Study of Photographer and Subject in Images of Native Americans', *Exposure*, 1991, XXVIII, 3: 23–33

Index

Alaska Native Brotherhood 35
American Anthropological
    Association 85
American Horse 84
American Museum of Natural
    History 116
Anderson, John Alvin 29–33, *29–30,
    32, 42, 45–9*
    Among the Sioux 31
    Sioux Memory Gems 32
Angeline, 'Princess' *108*
Anthropological Society of
    Washington 79

Barry, David F. 13, *11, 15*
Bass, William Wallace 36
Battle of the Little Bighorn 80, 104,
    113, *155*
Beals, Jesse Tarbox 85
Bear Ghost (Crow/Creek/Dakota) *146*
Bear's Belly (Arikara) *99*
Beautiful Hill (Omaha) *79*
Black Eagle (Assiniboin) *165*
Blackmore, William Henry 18, 21–2
Blackmore Museum 21
Blue Thunder, Katie (Brule Dakota) *42*
Boas, Franz 113, 115–6
Bogy, Lewis 21
Brady, Mathew 21–2
Bratley, Jesse Hastings 82
Broca, Paul 78
Bureau of American Ethnology
    (Smithsonian Institution) 22, 81–2,
    84, 112–13
Bureau of Indian Affairs (Office of
    Indian Affairs) 19–20

Catlin, George 17–18, 20–21, *25*
Chief Joseph (Nez Perce) 113, *15*
Columbia, Nancy *93*
Coudahwot *54, 57*
Cross, William R. 29–30
Cunningham, Imogene 112
Curly 104
Curley Bear (Blackfoot) *120*
Curtis, Ashael 108, 110
Curtis, Edward S. (Sheriff) 13, 22,
    102, 107–8, 110–17, *15, 99, 108,
    114, 148, 150, 153, 155–7, 159–
    65, 167–8, 170*
    In the Land of the Headhunters
    (film) 115–16, *114*
Curtis and Guptill 107

Davis, Richard (Cheyenne) *97*
Delegations 17, 19, 21–2, 78, 105,
    17, 23, 27
DeMille, Cecil B. 116
    The Ten Commandments (film)
    116
Dixon, Joseph Kossuth 13, 102–7,
    117, *104, 134–5, 137, 139–40,
    142–4, 146*
    The Vanishing Race 103, *146*
Dixon, Rollin Lester 103–5
    Hiawatha (film) 103
Dutro, Daniel 100

Eagle of Delight (Oto) *23*
Eastman, Mary 20
    *Dahcotah; or, Life and Legends
    of the Sioux Around Fort
    Snelling* 20
Eastman, Seth 19–20, *25*
Eaton, Edric 11, *11*
Emma (Kickapoo) *134*
EXPOSITIONS and WORLD
    FAIRS: 77–86
    Colonial Exposition (Amsterdam
    1883) 78
    Columbia Historical Exposition
    (Madrid) 81
    Crystal Palace (London, 1851) 78, 81
    International Centennial
    Exposition 80
    Jardin d'Acclimation Exposition
    (Paris, 1883) 78, *86*
    Louisiana Purchase Exposition
    (St Louis, Missouri, 1904) 13,
    85, 113, *77, 90, 93–4, 97*
    Panama–Pacific Exposition
    (San Francisco, California, 1915)
    102, 106, *126, 135*
    1889 Paris Universal Exposition 78
    Trans-Mississippi and
    International Exposition
    (Omaha, Nebraska, 1898) 13,
    81–5, *82, 89*
    World Columbian International
    Exposition 80–1, *93*

Field Columbian Museum (Field
    Museum) 40, *97*
Flaherty, Robert 115
    Nanook of the North
    (film) 115
Fletcher, Alice 82

Fool Bull (Brule Dakota) *45*
Forgetting (Apache) *89*

Gardner, Alexander *22, 26*
Gerhard Sisters (Mamie and Emma)
    13, 85–6, *8, 77, 90, 93–4, 97*
Geronimo 84–5, 114, *8*
Glover, Ridgway 11
Goes Ahead 104, 113
Goddard, Pliny Earl 116
Goff, Orlando Scott *15*
Good Voice (Brule Dakota) *47*
Grinnell, George Bird 110–11
Guptill, Thomas 107–8

Hairy Moccasin 104, 113
Hall, Judge James (*see also*
    McKenney and Hall) 19
Hard Chief (Omaha) *86*
Harriman, Edward H. (and
    Expedition) 102, 110–11
Harrison, Joseph 18
Haskayelthnaga (Navaho) *135*
Hayden, Ferdinand V. (*see also*
    SURVEYS) 21–2
Haynes, Frank J. 13, *15*
He Dog (Brule Dakota) *29*
Henry, Joseph 18, 21
Hillers, John K. 80–1
Hodge, Frederick Webb 11
Holding Eagle (Gros Ventre) *137*
Holmes, Burton 40
Horse Capture (Atsina) *156*
Horse Capture, George 41, 117
Hunt, George 114–16

Improved Order of Red Men
    (I.O.R.M.) 83
Indian Rights Association 83
Inverarity, Duncan 108, 110

Jackson, William Henry 22, 40, 80–
    82, 86
    Jackson catalogues 22
James, George Wharton 29, 36–40,
    37, 60, 62–3, 65–7
    *The Mokis and Their Snake
    Dance* 38
    *What the White Man May
    Learn from the Indian* 38
Jumping Eagle, Nellie (Dakota) *90*

Keokuk (Sac and Fox) *25*
Kills Two, Sam (Brule Dakota) *45*
King, Charles Bird 19–20, *17, 23, 26*
Kramer Gallery, St Paul, Minnesota 103

La Roche, Frank 111
Latham, Edward 113
Long (Apache) *89*
Lummis, Charles Fletcher 37

Many Coats (Navaho) *132*
Mason, Otis T. 80
Matteson, Sumner W., Jr. 29, 39–41,
    68, 70–74
Maude, Frederick H. 38
McBride, Ella 112
McClees, James Earle 21, 36, *27*
McGee, W. J. 85
McKenney, Thomas L. 19–20, *17*
McKenney and Hall *23*
McKinley, President William J. 81
Merriman, C. Hart 110
Monsen, Frederick 12, 37
Mooney, James 13, 82–3, 85
Morgan, J. Pierpont 102, 110, 114–15
Mountain Chief 105
Muhr, Adolph 13, 84–5, 112, *82, 89*

Nampeyo (Serpent Who Has No
    Teeth – Hano) *161*
No Heart (Iowa) *17*
Norris, Daisy (Blackfoot) *102, 125*
Not A Real Woman (Blackfoot) *119*

(Office of Indian Affairs *see* Bureau
    of Indian Affairs)
Oh-lo-ho-walla (Osage) 85, *94*
One Star (Brule Dakota) *48*

Parker, Quanah 114
Petalashara (Pawnee) *27*
Pierce, C. C. 38
Pierce, President Franklin 80
Plenty Coups 106
Pond, Percy *see* Winter and Pond
Powell, John Wesley 81
Prince Albert (consort of Queen
    Victoria) 78
Prince Roland Bonaparte 78–80, 86,
    79, 86

Peaux Rouges 79

Queen Victoria 78

Red Cloud (Oglala Dakota) 81, 84, 107, *148*
Red Cloud, Jack (Oglala Dakota – son of Red Cloud) 104, *137*
Red Hawk 105
Reed, Roland 13, 99–102, 117, *2–3, 101, 119–20, 122, 125–6, 129, 131–3*
Reifel, Ben (Brule Dakota) 31, *32*
Rinehart, Alfred Evan 82
Rinehart, Frank 13, 82–6, *82, 89*
   Rinehart's Indians 82
Roosevelt, President Theodore 39, 41, 106, 114
Runs the Enemy 104

'San Diego' *94*
Savage and Ottinger 11, *11*
Schoolcraft, Henry Rowe 20, *25*
   Indian Tribes of the United States 20
Schultz, James Willard 101
   Blackfoot Tales of Glacier National Park 101, *101*
Scott, General Winfield 80
Seattle (Chief Seattle/Siahl) *108*
Shindler, Antonio Zeno 21–2
   Shindler Catalogue 22
Shunkapaug 77
Shotridge, George (Yeilgoozu) 34, *57*
Sitting Bull (Hunkpapa Dakota) 81, *11*
Slow Bull (Oglala Dakota) *155*
Smithsonian Institution (*see also* Bureau of American Ethnology) 18, 20–22, 79–83, 112, *26*

Standing Bear (Omaha) 86
Stanley, John Mix 20, *26*
Stevenson, Matilda Coxe 113
SURVEYS:
   United States Geographical and Geological Survey of the Rocky Mountain Region ('Powell Survey') 80
   United States Geological and Geographical Survey of the Territories ('Hayden Survey') 21–2, 80
   United States Geological Survey 22

Taft, President William Howard 103, 105
Takes Five (Crow) *146*
Taylor, Frank E. 12, *14*
Tin-Tin-Meetsa (Umatilla) *146*
Trucha (Apache) *97*
Turning Bear (Brule Dakota) *46*
Two Moons *104*

Umapine (Cayuse) *146*

Vroman, Adam Clark 37, 40, 112

Wanamaker, Rodman (and Expeditions) 13, 102–7, *134–5, 137, 139–40, 142–4, 146*
Watson and Forbes
   The People of India 22
White, John 81
Whitehurst, Jesse 21
White-Man-Runs-Him 104, 113
Williams, Roy E. 102
Wilson, President Woodrow 104–05
Winter and Pond 29, 33–6, *34, 51–2, 54, 56–7, 59*

Winter, Lloyd *see* Winter and Pond
Wittick, George Ben 40
Wolf Robe (Cheyenne) *82*
Wounded Knee 12, 83, 113

Yellow Hair (Brule Dakota) *42*
Yeilgoozu *see* Shotridge, George

TRIBAL LISTING OF PLATES

NOTE In selecting the images for this publication, no attempt has been made to include all of the major tribes. Rather, the selection reflects those tribes recorded by the various photographers. Tribal designations, when known, are shown below even if not noted in captions. Many tribes are divided into smaller groups, or have differing names. For the purposes of this index, only major tribal designations have been used, and entries are under only one name variation as follows:

Apsaroke *see* Crow
Chilkat *see* Tlingit
Ojibway *see* Chippewa
Piegan *see* Blackfoot
Quagyuhl *see* Kwakiutl
Sioux *see* Dakota

TRIBE	PAGE NUMBER
Apache	8, 89, 97
Arikara	99
Assiniboin	68, 70–71, 150, 165
Atsina	156
Blackfoot	89, 101–2, 119–20, 122, 125, 140, 143, 167
Cayuse	146
Chemehuevi	66
Cheyenne	82, 97
Chippewa	2–3
Creek	146
Crow	139, 146, 164
Dakota	11, 25, 29–30, 32, 42, 45–9, 90, 137, 146, 148, 153, 155
Eskimo	93
Gros Ventre	68, 70–71, 137
Hano	161
Hopi	37, 60, 62–3, 65, 72–4, 133, 170
Iowa	17
Kickapoo	134
Kwakiutl	114, 168
Koskimo	168
Navaho	15, 90, 126, 131–2, 135, 153, 162
Nespilim	159
Nez Perce	15
Omaha	86
Osage	94
Oto	23
Pawnee	27
Quilcene	159
Sac and Fox	25
Shoshoni	12
Spokan	157
Tlingit	34, 51–2, 56–7, 59
Umatilla	146
Yuki	148